To Ker -
a behind the scene
shaker and mover!
Love,
Raggedy Joe
3/19/2007

"Like all women, I have experienced the freefall of transition about 'what's next'—but also the fulfillment that Dale affirms throughout this book. In many ways, my second calling is the most meaningful thing I have ever done. I can change the world in a different way now. So can every woman."

GENERAL CLAUDIA KENNEDY
Retired Deputy Chief of Staff for Army Intelligence and the first woman to achieve the rank of three-star general in the U.S. Army

"I loved this book. It takes everything our culture tells us about a woman's worth and turns it on its head—right side up. When we are being told that our best days are over, Dale reminds us that in God's kingdom the best is yet to be. If you are tired of running through your life, here is an invitation to be still and hear God's second calling. It will change your life and, by God's grace, change our world."

SHEILA WALSH
Women of Faith speaker and author of
I'm Not Wonder Woman but God Made Me Wonderful

"This is the book I have prayed for ten years God would lead someone to write—an articulate, authentic *Halftime* book for women. Women are different—thank God! Different priorities. Different tensions. Living in a different time. Dale Hanson Bourke gets it just right in *Second Calling*."

BOB BUFORD
Author of Halftime *and* Finishing Well *and founder of Leadership Network*

"A serious but witty book full of hope for any woman with any doubt that God has a purpose and plan for the back half of her life."

PEGGY WEHMEYER
Host of World Vision Report

"*Second Calling* is a wonderful book for women such as me who are navigating a life landscape filled with physical, emotional, familial, and spiritual change. For those of us in a season of shifting priorities and purposes, Dale Hanson Bourke affirms our desire for continued service and significance—and shares how we can discover anew that with God, the best truly is yet to come!"

JANE JOHNSON STRUCK
Editor of Today's Christian Woman *magazine*

"This book made me uncomfortable. That's saying a lot. Usually I can tell where an author is headed and get there before they do, thus insulating myself from the surprise that results in having to consider change. But Dale wound me in with her honest, human confessions so much that by the time she rounded certain corners in her self examination and spiritual processing, I went with her.

"Rats. Now I have to be different. Note that verb: not *do* something different. That would be somehow easier. Now I have to *be* different in the second half of my life . . . Thanks, Dale."

ELISA MORGAN
President and CEO of MOPS International

"My heart resonates with Dale Bourke's heart as she shares midlife hunger for more of God. Whatever your season of life, you will be blessed and spurred on to seek Him with more of your heart."

DENALYN LUCADO
Pastor's wife, mother of three, and author

"Like a good friend, Dale peels back her personal-life layers to reveal a timely message of clarity. I loved how she wove Naomi's story into relevant insights for me. [*Second Calling* is] an encouraging must-read for all of us who want to see what God has in store for the rest of our lives! Relevant. Real. Honest."

JOANI SCHULTZ
Chief Creative Officer of Group Publishing

"I wholeheartedly recommend *Second Calling*. I love Dale's insight that midlife offers women a 'holy break' and the opportunity to forge a new identity that is grounded in prayer and is world-changing in scope. On every page of this wise and well-crafted book I found both affirmation and challenge. I sincerely hope that millions of midlife women will read *Second Calling*, become convinced that the best is yet to come, and make themselves fully available to a new work of God in and through them. As Dale says, together we can bring the Kingdom of God to earth in every imaginable way."

LYNNE HYBELS
Willow Creek Community Church
Author of Nice Girls Don't Change the World

"In a culture that endlessly reminds women my age that we are 'past our prime,' Dale shows us that God's plans for us are just beginning. In giving us a new perspective of the life of Naomi, she also gives us courage to let go of those things that once defined us, and to embrace God's second calling on our lives."

RENEE' STEARNS
Former attorney, wife, mother of five, and speaker on women's issues and the poor

"*Second Calling* will serve as a wonderful resource to the thousands of individuals seeking to answer God's call on their lives. At Bridgestar, we work every day with men and women, secular and faith-based, who are asking 'what's next?' in looking for senior management jobs in the nonprofit sector—many after successful careers in business, government, or returning to work after raising a family. If you want to embrace the second half of your life with passion, power and purpose, *Second Calling* will help you take a big first step. Enjoy!"

DAVID SIMMS
Managing Partner of Bridgestar, an initiative of The Bridgespan Group

"Dale's honest self-reflection encouraged me to do the same. I appreciated her invitation to pause and consider mid-course adjustments for the second half of life. The challenge to realign priorities around relationships and activities that will have lasting impact was communicated as one spiritual wrestler to another. I found Dale's insights from the book of Ruth and stories from the lives of contemporary friends to be compelling examples of commitment to eternal significance."

LAURA CROSBY
Speaker and creator of "Cross-training," a ministry of spiritual mentoring at Christ Presbyterian Church, Edina, MN

"YES! As a woman definitely in the 'second half of life,' I found myself identifying deeply with Dale's excitement about the possibilities. Not 'doing' more, but going deeper, having more to give. The subtitle says it all: passion and purpose for the rest of my life. It doesn't get better than that! Sisters, we need to help one another discover our 'second calling.'"

NETA JACKSON
Author of The Yada Yada Prayer Group *fiction series*

second calling

second calling

finding passion & purpose
for the rest of your life

DALE HANSON BOURKE

Second Calling

Published by Integrity Publishers, a division of Integrity Media, Inc.
5250 Virginia Way, Suite 110 Brentwood, TN 37027.

HELPING PEOPLE WORLDWIDE EXPERIENCE *the* MANIFEST PRESENCE *of* GOD.

Published in association with Alive Communications, Inc., 7680 Goddard
Street Suite 200, Colorado Springs, CO 80920.

Some names and details have been changed to respect the privacy of people
whose personal stories are shared in this book.

Unless otherwise indicated, Scripture quotations are taken from *The Message*
by Eugene H. Peterson. Copyright © 1993, 1994, 1995, 1996, 2000, 2001,
2002. Used by permission of NavPress Publishing Group. All rights reserved.

Scripture references marked KJV are taken from the King James Version of the
Bible. Public domain.

Cover Design: Brand Navigation, LLC—DeAnna Pierce, Bill Chiaravalle,
www.brandnavigation.com
Cover Photo: The Image Bank—Shaun Egan
Interior Design: Susan Browne Design
Author Photo: Tyler J. Bourke

ISBN 1-59145-332-1

Printed in the United States of America
06 07 08 09 10 BVG 8 7 6 5 4 3 2 1

To Peggy Wehmeyer Woods
and
Linda LeSourd Lader,
my friends and fellow travelers
on this journey of the soul.

contents

acknowledgments

This book would never have been written without the prayers, words of encouragement, cups of coffee, and open hearts of so many of my friends. Thanks to the women in my Community Bible Study group (led so graciously by Sharon Ekdahl), who shared a unique adventure in studying the Gospel of John and encouraging one another. Thanks, too, to Pam Kellogg Green, who is a generous, wise, and caring friend and who prayed this book to completion. Linda and Peggy, to whom this book is dedicated, should probably have their names on the front cover. Without them, there wouldn't be a book.

My agent, Rick Christian, helped me not only work out the business side of this book but also provided invaluable guidance on the tone and substance. My "old" friends at Integrity—Byron, Joey, Laura, Rob—and my "new" friends, Kris, Scott, LaVenia, and others, have provided me with the atmosphere of stability, encouragement, and professionalism that most writers only dream of in a publisher. I am grateful for all the experiences we have shared over the decades and the conversations not only about publishing but also about life. Thanks to Bruce Barbour for friendship and publishing guidance over the many, many years. And special thanks to Jennifer Stair, whom I would like to hire to edit my entire life.

So many others have given me just the right word when I struggled or shared an experience or a quote or a prayer. Thanks to Linda Wilkinson, Betsy West, Nancy Low, Emily Cothran, Renee Stearns, Lourine Clark, Carrie Slease, Mary McClymont, Janet Hall, Cheryl Martin, Pamela Barden, Margaret Cudney, Kay Warren, and Lynne Hybels.

And finally, to my boys, Tom, Chase, and Tyler, you have loved me through the experiences of this book and through the days when writing replaced cooking, cleaning, and anything resembling civilized life. You have believed in me, encouraged me, and defended me. Thank you, and I love you.

1. a new day dawning

Somewhere between the memories of what has been and the hopes of what might be, we pause, take a deep breath, and wonder. Until that moment, we have charged forward, propelled by circumstances and opportunities toward what felt like a limitless beyond. We dreamed with abandon, first on our own behalf and then on behalf of our children. "Anything is possible," we told ourselves.

But now, as we pause in our middle years, we begin to see some boundaries. Optimism is tempered by realism. The wild dreams are no longer goals. The limitless hopes give way to quiet acceptance of facts. We begin to tally our wins and losses, and we assess that we have been more fortunate than most. "It's not so bad," we tell ourselves.

In the act of taking stock, we realize how much we have changed. We no longer abandon the past like a change of clothes. We pick it up, examine it, and hold it a little closer.

And as we look forward, we do so with a bit of hesitation. We know from experience that the future is not always our friend.

It is in this parenthesis, this time of reflection, that we are so very vulnerable. We are now at a point of reevaluation. We are in a moment when, whether we realize it or not, our future will be marked by what we have come to believe.

Listen to the market, and you will learn what you must consume in order to continue to have value. Take vitamins, color your hair, and prop up your hormones. Do these things to stave off the inevitability of waking up to discover you are older.

But listen to your heart, and you will learn something else. You are softer, gentler, wiser, and calmer than you have ever been. You are emerging from the whirlwind of your youth and seeing the present more clearly. You are becoming more fully and completely who you were created to be.

If you listen carefully, you will hear a whisper. It is not the cacophony of advertisers telling you to hide your fine lines and wrinkles. It is something far more pervasive and subtle. It is a whisper that says you are being called to something new. It is a gentle voice that seems to say, "Ah, now I have your attention." It is a voice that has been patiently waiting to speak truth you would be able to hear.

We are no longer in that part of life when we simply respond to parents, children, husbands, jobs, the PTA, and recycling schedules. We are not spending every single minute trying to keep everyone else happy. We are suddenly not so busy. In fact, we might even be feeling a little lonely. Where did all the noise and activity go? Where are all the people who once needed us? One day, we realize we are facing down the gaping abyss known as the second half of life.

If you are a Christian woman, as I am, and if you read the Bible, as I do, you may at some point begin to realize that if you listen hard enough, you hear something holy in that whisper. It is not a voice of doom but of promise. It is not about condemnation but about deliverance. It does not say that you are all washed up but that you are being baptized into a new life.

God, it turns out, doesn't really care if we are sagging or graying or aching. He doesn't care how much estrogen we have or whether our falling arches have moved us from stiletto heels to Birkenstocks. And here's a hot flash for us all: in God's economy, the fact that we are becoming less physically attractive may be just the way he wants us.

God is mostly concerned with one aspect of us: our hearts. He wants them to be in tip-top shape. He wants them strong, responsive, and enthusiastic, even if he has to wait until we are eighty and looking back fondly on the days of fine lines and wrinkles. But it would be a shame if he had to wait that long!

A FLASH FROM THE PAST

Looking back at my twenties and thirties, I'm not sure how I did it. Much of those years are a blur, but the following particular thirty-six hours stands out in my memory.

The client called just as I was serving dinner. I cradled the phone against my ear as I served the peas. *A last-minute emergency. Really need you to attend an important meeting in Los Angeles tomorrow.* My husband finished cutting our younger son's meat while I grabbed a pencil and paper and took notes.

I had the flight schedules from Washington, D.C., to Los Angeles memorized because I flew the route so often. I knew I could catch the 7 a.m. flight, rent a car, and be at the client's office by late morning. "No problem," I told the client, who promised to fax me information I could review on the flight. We finished dinner, I put the boys to bed, and then I called the airline and the rental car company. I booked a morning flight and a red-eye return flight for the next day. I'd meet with the client all afternoon, drive back to the airport, and fly through the night. If all went well, I'd be back in time to drive carpool the following day. I went to bed and set my alarm for five hours later in order to get up and catch the flight. I'd try to catch a nap on the plane.

The airplane was somewhere over the Midwest when I remembered: I was room mother for my older son's class, and they were having a St. Patrick's Day party the next day. If I ended up staying overnight, they wouldn't have decorations. Thank heavens for overnight deliveries! After renting a car in Los Angeles, I drove to a mall, filled a box with green party decorations, and then stopped at a Federal Express office. I scribbled the teacher's name and the school address on the box and checked the square to be sure it was delivered first thing in the morning. Just in case I had to stay over, I'd still fulfill my duties as room mother.

It all worked out. The meeting went well, and the client launched a new project with my company. The flight back arrived too late for me to drive carpool, but my husband filled in, as he often did. The decorations were hand-delivered to the school, not by me but by a man in a uniform. I drove to the office from the airport, did several hours of work, and then went home, cooked dinner, and went to bed as soon as my children fell asleep.

Looking back on those days, I can only think I was out of my mind. But at the time, I really thought I had it figured out. I was running a company, traveling so often that the people at the airport knew me by name, driving carpool, cooking (or at least thawing) dinner, and taking my turn as room mother, among many other responsibilities. My life was whizzing by at such a fast pace that I'm not sure I appreciated much of it. I did have help, though. My husband deserved a medal for taking on so much, we had a regular baby-sitter who was always on call, and I had a terrific and energetic staff who were willing to jump in on any project, personal or professional.

If you had asked, and if I had found the time to reflect at all, I might have said that I felt called to each of my roles. I loved being a mom. And being a good mom meant taking my turn driving carpool and being a room mother. I was the owner of a company and had a dozen people depending on me for their incomes. I had several clients, each with compelling missions that drove their organizations. I was also a wife, daughter, church member, and board director. I did not understand how my own needs and addictions propelled me forward, nor did I realize that every opportunity was not necessarily a calling.

As it is for many women, the first half of my life was centered on family. But I was also part of the generation that believed we could have it all, and many of us just about killed ourselves trying. We worked because doors opened to us for the first time, because we had been well educated and encouraged not to "waste" our education, and because the lifestyle we wanted to live required the income from two careers. We had been given choices at the great buffet of life, and many of us decided to take "one of each."

Bob Buford has helped many men make the transition into the second half of life through his books *Halftime* and *Game Plan*.[1] I've read both books and have learned a great deal from them. Anyone who has been very career-focused in the first half of life will benefit from Bob's wisdom and encouragement.

One of Bob's themes is that we must move "from success to significance" in the second half of life. I can't count the number of men who have quoted that phrase to me with something like awe at how well it sums up their desire. Rich Stearns, the current president of World Vision, and Chris Crane, the president of Opportunity International, are two men who left extremely successful business careers to become heads of ministries. I have heard each of these men admit that they consider themselves to be examples of individuals who heard a godly call in that direction.

But there is something about that phrase—"from success to significance"—that does not quite relate to most women I know in the same way. Most of us, whether career-oriented or not, found significance in the first half of our lives in relationships. Nothing about my career or other activities holds a candle to how I feel about being a wife and mother. Few of us experience either the satisfaction or heartache over work that we invest in our children or our other relationships.

Something else is going on with women, I'm convinced. God may be calling men from success to significance, but I believe he is calling women to something not only significant but far more revolutionary—and possibly less definable. He wants more of us—and less. He wants us to know that the best is not behind us. God is calling us from others to him. He wants more of us than we can even imagine because he wants to do more *through* us than we could possibly know.

I believe God has a special purpose for women in the second half of life that is world-changing in its scope. If we can understand what God is calling us to and can turn away from those voices calling us to stay attached to our youth, we will be given a power and purpose beyond anything we have experienced.

FINDING PERSPECTIVE

For twenty-one years, I have been meaning to put our family photos into a proper photo album instead of keeping them in the dozens of boxes that have accumulated and spilled out of the cabinet next to the television. Before our sons leave home for good, I want each of them to have an album of memories. This photo album project has become a labor of love.

Now that I am no longer running to games every weekend or standing watch over homework, I have time to actually take in all those days that once rushed by us. I have time to look through all the boxes of photos, searching the faces of the boys at each birthday party to see big smiles

and occasional pouts. Our vacation photos show us looking young, happy, and relaxed.

My husband and I are sitting in the family room as I sort
through two decades of snapshots. Every few minutes, I interrupt my husband's reading and hand him a photo. Chase,
looking in terror at the clown we had hired to entertain him
and his friends on his birthday. Tyler, mugging for the cam-
era, already showing signs of the actor he will become. More
than twenty years of family life. Sometimes my husband
chuckles as I show him a snapshot. Sometimes he smiles
sadly, like when I discover the picture of his father sitting
with his uncle and our two boys sitting in front of them.
Granddad Bourke and Uncle Bill have both passed away.

Our little boys are now men. Our older son, Chase, is
twenty-one as I write, a legal adult, living away at college.
His seventeen-year-old brother, Tyler, who has shoulders as
wide as the doorway, is upstairs doing his homework and
preparing to take his SAT exam. He'll be leaving for college
soon. There is no doubt that they are no longer little boys.
Time has passed faster than we can even comprehend.

It was a crazy life, but it was a good life. I could have
baked more cakes from scratch, spent more time reading
bedtime stories, and created better holiday decorations.
But I don't have any huge regrets. The first half of my life
was a whirl of activity, a series of new projects, a bustle

of anticipation. I never seemed to have enough time, although I now marvel at all the things I felt I *had* to do. I was in such a hurry to build a résumé, add to our savings account, get my sons on the right track, find the perfect vacation spot, and be the best at every role I took on.

I am working on the photo books when it strikes me: *I was in a hurry to get here.* All of those hectic, crazy days brought me to where I am now. If a client called me today and asked me to be in Los Angeles tomorrow, I would just laugh.

There was all that noise then, and now there's so much silence. And in that silence, perhaps a sense that God is calling us to him. He has waited patiently as we raised children, built a résumé, and scurried about building our lives. He has always been there, of course, but most of us fit him in around all the other aspects of our lives. Then we come to a point when something is different. We naturally fear the sense of loss. As we realize that we have decades ahead of us, we also begin to wonder how to fill them. What will we do?

Here's what I am learning: God wants us to spend the second half of our lives worrying less about what we do and more about who we become. He wants to turn our lives upside down and use us in magnificent, unexpected, world-changing ways. He is mobilizing an army of women who have unprecedented health, wealth, and education.

He is calling us to step up to the challenge and to leave the past behind.

The psychologist Carl Jung observed, "But we cannot live the afternoon of life according to the program of life's morning—for what was great in the morning will be little at evening, and what in the morning was true will at evening be a lie."[2]

If you are in or approaching the second half of your life, this book is for you. It contains no beauty tips or slimming secrets. It does not contain any advice on facelifts, liposuction, or tummy tucks. You can do all or none of those things, and it really doesn't matter. This is about heart work. God is calling you to build spiritual muscle, to develop a résumé of soul work, to find peace and joy like you have never known. God wants to take you on an adventure unlike anything you have ever dreamed. "He will whisper to us not in the mad rush and fever of our striving and our fierce determination to be someone," wrote Emilie Griffin, "but rather when we are content to rest in him, to put ourselves into his keeping, into his hands."[3]

HAVING IT ALL

I was sitting on an elevated stage, one of ten women between the ages of forty-five and seventy. We were here to talk about lessons we learned about "having it all." The other panelists were all very accomplished women: a judge, a partner in a major law firm, the owner of a television station. We were attending a four-day event that brought people together from all over the country and from various backgrounds to talk about everything from international security risks to spiritual lessons. Panels were assigned, and I wondered why I was on this one. Everyone else seemed so much more accomplished, so much better at really having it all. I felt like an imposter.

But then the stories began to emerge. The businesswoman whose breast cancer gave her a new appreciation for life. The "perfect mother" who became an accomplished artist after her children left home. The television producer who nurtured her love of gardening into a second career. The engineer whose husband had become an ambassador and who now made a career of hosting receptions and representing her country.

We all had stories. No matter what we had done in the first half of life, we saw the second half differently. It didn't matter if we had been homemakers or judges. We each, in our own way, felt a call to something different in the second half of life. Some had reached that conclusion through trauma, such as illness, divorce, or the death of a loved one. Others simply described it as an awakening. Said one woman, "I woke up one day and wondered what I had been thinking all those years." I don't know how much the audience appreciated our musings, but we all had a great time.

When the session was over, we stayed on the platform and talked to each other until they chased us out of the room so the next session could start. Our paths might never have crossed in the first half of our lives. But where we stood, at the dawning of the second half, we had everything in common.

A SECOND-HALF WOMAN

Naomi would have fit right in with the group of women on that platform—Naomi from the Book of Ruth in the Old Testament, that is. I had begun to study her a few months before, learning from her example as a woman whom God had used to accomplish his will. I had developed a certain kinship with Naomi I had never before experienced with a biblical character.

Naomi is the archetypal second-half-of-life woman. When we meet her in the Book of Ruth, she is firmly planted in midlife. She has gone from a full first half of life to an empty future. Life is so bad that she announces she was changing her name to Mara, which means "bitter."

But God called Naomi in midlife, just as he called me and is calling you. He promised her something more than she had ever imagined if she would trust him in the second half of her life. She did, and despite losing her entire family, the story ends as she is called the grandmother of baby Obed, who later becomes the grandfather of David.

Naomi became part of the greatest story ever told, not because of what she did in the first half of her life but because of what God did through her in the second half. In a few short chapters of the Bible, she moves from tragedy to miraculous victory and an ending far beyond anything Naomi would have written for herself.

A MODERN NAOMI

General Claudia Kennedy was the first woman to achieve the rank of three-star general in the U.S. Army. She is attractive, feminine, and tough. She was successful in a man's world at a time when it wasn't popular to be a woman in the military, moving up the ranks to become Deputy Chief of Staff for Army Intelligence.

When Claudia retired at fifty-three, she officially entered the second half of her life. No more uniforms, orders, or mess halls. But she also lost the camaraderie of the military and the community from which she drew friends. "Getting involved with Opportunity International saved my life," she says.

After speaking at an event for the Christian microfinance organization, she became more involved in the ministry, visiting the Dominican Republic and seeing women who had received small loans pulling themselves out of poverty. Claudia now spends much of her time speaking on behalf of the organization and using her military intelligence background to help explain why we should "make peace" by helping people find economic freedom. "If you had told me I would be doing something like this ten years ago, I would have laughed," she says. "But in many ways, this is the most meaningful thing I have ever done in my life. It's not a career so much as a calling."

I can't imagine under what circumstances I would have ever met a general during my first fifty years or what I would have said to one if I had. But I think of Claudia as a friend, not because of her great accomplishments in the first half of life but because of her open heart today. We both care deeply about the poor of the world, especially women who have never had the same opportunities we experienced. Our paths would never have crossed in the first half of life, yet we share so much in this season. Our pasts have brought us to a place where our résumés gather dust and our accomplishments are only experiences and memories. Claudia and other women I know are interested in changing the world in a different way.

My friend Emily doesn't have the luxury of contemplating retirement. She's the single mother of an adult daughter and must support herself. We've known each other for years and once spent much of our time talking about the latest news in the publishing world. But now Emily and I seem to spend more of our time talking about other things.

Even though she works full time, Emily also volunteers at the local hospital, helping parents of chronically ill children. She is especially good at this, because twenty-five years ago, she was one of those parents. Emily feels called to spend much of her free time helping parents who are suffering through this difficult time, partially because she understands their pain and partially because it helps her honor the memory of the infant daughter she lost. I have no doubt that her support and counsel to those parents is some of the most significant work Emily has ever done. Emily is one of the most empathetic people I know because the pain she suffered in the first half of her life didn't make her bitter, but it taught her how to comfort others.

A second calling isn't about something you do but about someone you become. It is the belief that the best is yet to come, and it will probably look very different than anything that has come before. It is faith that God's call is not just for the young but for the faithful. It is the confidence that what we can do through God is more than we can imagine accomplishing on our own. Your second calling doesn't necessarily build your résumé, but it builds your soul.

In this book, you'll read more about Naomi because her life is evidence that God wants to tell a story through us as well. And you'll meet more women like Claudia and Emily —bright, energetic women who are embracing the second half of life with passion and purpose. Mostly, I hope you will also meet yourself through this book. Not the woman you have been, but the woman God is calling you to be.

If that sounds frightening, remember the words of Isaiah 43:18–19: "Forget about what's happened; don't keep going over old history. Be alert, be present. I'm about to do something brand-new. It's bursting out! Don't you see it? There it is! I'm making a road through the desert, rivers in the badlands."

2. getting personal

Naomi must have thought she had it made. After all, she was married to a great guy who not only loved her but also loved God. He came from a good, respected family: hard workers, God followers, landowners. Their marriage was blessed with not one but two sons to carry on the name, inherit the land, and care for her in her old age. She had everything a woman of her day could have hoped for.

And her husband wasn't passive, either. When a famine came to Judah, he loaded up Naomi and the boys and headed for greener pastures in a place called Moab, which was not very far away from their home, yet far enough to seem exotic. The Moabites weren't enemies—they welcomed Naomi's family—but they weren't exactly like the Israelites, either. For one thing, they worshiped a different god; they weren't people of the covenant. So when Naomi's sons both fell in love with Moabite women, this must have created a bit of a stir. Yet somehow, even in that, Naomi seemed blessed. She adored both of her daughters-in-law, and they revered her. There must have been a time when Naomi sat back and thought, *It doesn't get any better than this.*

Before the Book of Ruth begins, Naomi is enjoying a wonderful life. She is middle-aged and content. She loves God and her family, and all seems right in the world.

Then the bottom falls out of her peaceful world. Her husband dies, and then her two sons are killed. We don't know how. We don't even know whether it was murder or an accident or disease. But whatever the case, in a relatively short period of time, Naomi lost everything that was dear to her. She still had her daughters-in-law, but she knew if they stayed with her, their lives would be ruined. So early in the Book of Ruth, Naomi assesses the situation. She has gone from being the most fortunate, blessed woman she knew to being a helpless, grieving widow.

Although the book is named after Naomi's daughter-in-law, Ruth, this is, in many ways, the story of Naomi. The story begins with all the markings of a tragedy. But through divine providence and Naomi's obedience, the Book of Ruth ends just four chapters later with Naomi not only feeling fulfilled but playing a pivotal role in the fulfillment of prophecy. She goes from being in the pits to becoming one of the most important women in the Bible. And she does it in ways that every woman can understand and emulate.

In studying this book, I have come to love Naomi. I identify with her and want to be like her. Why? Because she is, in many ways, the example to all of us women who have reached a certain age. It's not a particular year or month. It's just that time in life when a woman starts to feel that she is getting older, that she's no longer a kid. For some women it comes at forty; for others, it may be sixty. Whenever it is, the realization somehow surprises us. And at first, at least, it is not a good surprise.

In her book *Necessary Losses*, Judith Viorst puts it this way: "We feel shaken. We feel scared. We do not feel safe. The center's not holding and things are falling apart. . . . We inspire far less lust than we do respect. We're not quite prepared to settle for only respect."[1]

Whatever the physical manifestations of aging—whether it's the first wrinkle, the first gray hair, or the first hot flash—there is a sense of betrayal. *What's happening to my body? Who is doing this to me?* I find myself recalling the days when I could run three miles without getting tired or stay up all night and still go to work the next day. It's not that I still want to do those things. It's just that I wonder when they became memories, not possibilities.

Even if all is going well in life, we can still identify in one way or another with Naomi, who realizes that at her age she can no longer start over. No one will marry her, she's too old to start another family, she can't inherit the land of her husband, and she's in a foreign country. Her options are extremely limited.

In our culture, things are considerably better in some ways. Most women can earn a living or inherit property from our birth family. But the fact is, there are many things we can no longer do after we turn forty that we once took for granted. And at some point, if we are truly honest, we feel a little angry about the way aging women are viewed. We dye our hair, buy creams and lotions, and even take a variety of medications and herbal products promising some form of the fountain of youth.

The problem is, we are still getting old. There's simply no way to stop the process. So here's the first thing we can learn from Naomi: let it out. Go ahead and have yourself a good yell. In fact, go ahead and give God a piece of your mind. That's what Naomi did, and who could blame her?

Naomi's life had gone from a Norman Rockwell scene to something resembling Picasso's *Guernica*. God had waited until she was middle-aged, no longer valued for her sex appeal or childbearing capacity, to radically change her life. Naomi did not, for one moment, stop believing in God. Instead she completely, and without reservation, blamed him for taking away everything she held dear. "GOD has dealt me a hard blow," she says (Ruth 1:13).

There is, on the surface, nothing good about aging. Not only do we look worse, but we feel worse. We begin to have aches and pains. We can't eat everything or do the things we loved. We become a shadow of who we once were. We can deny it, but denial is not the way God has asked us to live. Our other option is simply to let it out. Here's a suggestion: Write a prayer to God about aging. Let him know how you feel. It's OK. He can handle it. He knows already. Like Naomi, let God know how you feel about the blow he has dealt you.

Here's what I wrote in my journal one day:

> God, you know I never spent much time on my appearance. But you also know how much I liked it if men noticed me when I walked into the room. Maybe it was a sin then. Maybe it's a sin to miss it. But I do. I miss being able to turn heads. I miss being able to eat anything and not gain weight. I miss jumping out of bed in the morning and going for a long run. I don't like to look in the mirror and see my bags and wrinkles. I don't like that people hold the door for me and call me "ma'am," not "miss." I don't like that someone offered me a seat on the subway the other day. I don't like that my life seems less full of possibilities and more full of memories.

Perhaps I had spent too much time in the New Testament, studying women like Mary and Martha and the woman at the well. They are certainly women to be admired. But once I began to seriously study the Old Testament, I realized that women like Naomi were drawn in such richer terms, and I became fascinated. Perhaps they are so fully described because their actions and character are shaping the lineage of Jesus. Perhaps, despite the circumstances of their day, they were simply more fully and openly themselves.

The more I studied the story of Naomi—her actions, character, and example—the more I wanted to know her. Naomi, it seemed to me, could walk in to the twenty-first century and fit right in. She is strong, independent, and determined. She is no whiner, and she is certainly not a pushover. More than anything, she is a woman of God.

Naomi's relationship with God is amazingly personal. She never stops believing he has been responsible for everything that has happened in her life. She even threatens to change her name after she feels he has ruined her life. As we see the relationship between God and Naomi play out, we also see how very much God loves her and provides for her in a way that is truly miraculous. God knows what Naomi wants more than she does. And he gives it to her in a way that is far beyond anything she would have imagined. We can only look at this book and say it is a love story, not about Ruth and Naomi or Ruth and Boaz, but about Naomi and God.

One of the characteristics of Naomi is her boldness. Perhaps it was an attribute she expressed more fully after her husband and sons were gone. Now that she is alone in the world, she has no one to tell her to keep quiet. There is no one to embarrass, and she feels responsible not only for herself but also for Ruth. While she may be more passive on her own behalf, she is not going to let Ruth lose out.

AN AFRICAN NAOMI

Naomi reminds me of a woman I met in a small village in Africa. Several years ago, I was visiting a village in Senegal with a team from World Vision. World Vision had been working with villages in the region to help solve the health problems and discovered that many of the health issues related directly to the lack of clean water. It was not uncommon to see women walking through the dessert with buckets on their heads, scooping water out of fetid ponds left from the rainy season and taking it back to the village. The child mortality rate in such villages was staggering.

But in villages where wells had been dug, the situation changed dramatically. Children lived at a significantly increased rate and had fewer illnesses, as did the adults. With a well in the village, women spent less of their day walking back and forth to the ponds and had time to begin literacy training and to take better care of their families.

I visited two such villages with World Vision workers and saw firsthand the incredible health and lifestyle improvements that came with having a well. Then we visited a third village, where there was no well. The people in the village gathered around to meet the strange visitors. The head of our group met with the chief of the village, greeting him and asking polite questions. Finally, the discussion got down to business. The World Vision worker asked the chief about the number of children who were sick. The chief acknowledged there were many. He asked if many died, and the chief said yes. Finally, the worker asked about the water supply. The chief pointed to the distance and talked about a pond that was created during the rainy season.

The World Vision worker asked if the village knew about wells. The chief nodded and then pulled a tattered piece of paper out of the pocket of his robe. "We are getting a well," the translator interpreted for us. As the World Vision worker studied the piece of paper with a perplexed look, an older woman moved through the crowd to the front.

She began to speak clearly and directly, and some of the people began to murmur. The translator began to share her words with us. "I am an old woman and have no husband to keep me quiet, so I will speak up.

"I have watched the children of this village die for too many years. I have lost too many of my own. Many years ago, someone came and promised us a well. But he never came back. The chief here keeps telling us that a well is coming. He tells others who come to our village that we already have the promise of a well, because he does not want to lose face.

"But we have no well, and we are losing too many children. If you can help us, please come to this village. I do not want to watch any more children die." Having said what she needed to say, she then walked to the back of the group and sat down again.

The woman's words created something close to a riot in the village. Many said she should never have spoken to strangers, while others supported her and began to speak angrily to the chief.

I remember being struck by the woman's courage and clarity. And I also remember thinking that she had harnessed the power of her situation and used it for the good of others. She was past the point of worrying about how others viewed her. She had the freedom of having no husband to embarrass. Like Naomi, she spoke boldly.

That village finally got a well, probably because of her action. She may be gone now, but her legacy will live on. Many more children in that village will be alive for generations to come because one woman spoke up. She had the freedom and power that came with her age and place in the village. And she used it, not to advance herself but to help others.

MORE THAN ONE WOMAN

In her time, Naomi was a survivor just to have made it to her age. She had already survived a famine and the death of her husband and two sons. She had endured childbirth at least twice—something that took the lives of many women of her day. And even at her age, without any medical care, vitamins, or energy bars, she embarked upon the arduous journey back to Judah without hesitation.

Today, women aged forty and over make up more than half of the female population in America, according to the U.S. Census Bureau.[2] Almost twenty-two million are between the ages of forty and fifty, with another twenty million joining their ranks in the next decade. We represent an unprecedented population bulge, mostly known as the baby boomers.

We also represent an unprecedented level of health, education, and wealth in this country. Most of us started exercising regularly in grade school and kept up a fairly active life through college and beyond. That's one of the reasons my friend Laurie, who just turned sixty, has a size six figure and could easily pass for forty. She goes to the gym every day and has for more than thirty years. She also, like most women I know, finished college, has spent some years working and some being home with children, and has had excellent medical care. Those who chart these things can't be sure, of course, but they are expecting a surprisingly high number of women in our generation will live to the age of one hundred. Most of us will at least pass eighty.

This huge, unprecedented population movement makes me think that we have an opportunity unlike any group of women has ever faced. I keep thinking that if God could work so mightily through Naomi, what could he do with millions of Christian women who are healthy, wealthy, and wise? (Well, at least, well educated.)

Many of us are looking for something more than a job to fill our days. Even those of us who work find that we invest less of our identity in our job and more in the rest of our life. Many of us are seeking deeper spiritual roots. Take the case of Ann Fudge. A cover article for *BusinessWeek* reports, "After a quarter century as a rising star in corporate America and just one year after she had been promoted to run a $5 billion division of Kraft Foods, Inc., Fudge walked away. She didn't do it for her two sons, who were already grown and embarked upon careers of their own. . . . Like a number of her peers, she simply wanted to define herself by more than her professional status, considerable as it was, and financial rewards, sizable as they were."[3]

So what did Fudge do with her time? "It meant rising early to do yoga instead of racing to work, reading books about moving the soul instead of moving products." The article goes on to document the fact that corporate women are dropping out in unprecedented numbers around the age of fifty. Most, like Fudge, are doing so because they want more out of life.

If all these women are dropping out of the corporate world, and many women have ended their carpooling duties, what might God want to do with us? Think about it. If all the Christian women aged forty and older got truly serious about seeking God and letting him use us in amazing ways, we could completely change our world. We could certainly change our communities and help bring about revival in our churches. We could help bring stability to conflict zones, hold the hand of every person dying of AIDS in Africa, and eradicate world hunger. We could bring peace to many countries, teach literacy to anyone who wanted to read, and build houses for every homeless person in America. We could help bring the kingdom of God to earth in every imaginable way.

But our incredible opportunity would come with a few challenges. We would have to know God well and seek him as if our lives depended on it. We would have to eliminate the frivolous time wasters in our lives and focus on what was really important. We would have to wake up each day and ask God to show us what he wanted us to do. We would have to believe that God wanted to use the second half of our lives with more purpose, power, and passion than anything we ever achieved in the first half.

If millions and millions of women listened to that whisper and followed their second calling, it is simply breathtaking to think of what God could do. That's my dream. It has been a growing vision and a quiet stirring in my heart ever since I started studying the story of Naomi and saw what God was able to do through her. It is the dream that warmed my heart after it had grown empty and dusty from running hard after the wrong goals.

I believe that God wants to redeem all of the broken heels, chipped nails, dead-end jobs, broken marriages, less-than-perfect children, bad perms, fad diets, lost friendships, and PMS of the first half of our lives. He needed us to get those things out of the way. He was with us then, but he wants us to really be with him now. He wants us to trust in something so much bigger than the best diet, the most wonderful sale, the biggest house on the block, the finest china, the top title, even the perfect husband. He wants us to know that just as he can take a woman who feels bitter and empty to being full to overflowing, so, too, can he transform even our best lives into something so much more.

LISTENING TO THE WORLD

A few years after I met the woman in Senegal, I visited Bosnia with World Vision. We were planning a visit to a nearby village when we heard about a group of women and children who had been temporarily housed in a community center. Word was, these were survivors of Srebrenica, the village where a horrible atrocity had taken place: all the men and boys were murdered while they believed they were under UN protection. We wanted to see if we could find these women and help them in any way.

As we wound our way through mountain villages, we relied on the word of strangers who pointed us to a lovely spot in the shadow of a mountain. We drove up to the village and found the community building where all the village activities once took place, now full of women and children seeking shelter.

When my female translator and I walked into the room, we were shocked. Mattresses were lined up against the walls, and women and children seemed to be in every inch of the room. Someone was cooking on a small, portable burner. Many of the children were coughing and appeared sick. Some of the women looked so haggard and drawn, it was hard to imagine they could be the mothers of the children. Through our translator, we began to hear stories of the horrors these women and children had endured. Most begged us to try to find out what had happened to their husbands and sons. But in their eyes, we saw that most feared they would never see their loved ones again.

We sat and listened to these women tell us about the lives they had left and their fears for the future. They told us that the people in the village had been kind, but they knew they could not stay there forever. We asked what they needed, and they told us that they had blankets and warm clothes but, hesitatingly, they admitted that they had no underwear for themselves or their children. It was hard to wash every day, yet they wanted to be clean. They explained that as Muslims, it was hard for them to tell the men who had come about this, but they were glad that women had come to hear their story.

We cried as we left. We couldn't imagine what these women had gone through or how their lives would ever be made whole. But we knew that there was one thing we could do for them, and that was to get them underwear. We were determined to respond to their request.

My friend Karen Stockman mobilized the women in her Women of Vision chapter in Southern California. She began collecting new underwear and then trying to find someone who would fly it to Bosnia for us. (There were still no flights going into the country, so we had to arrange for a flight to Croatia and then have the supplies trucked in.) Within two weeks, she had five hundred pounds of under-wear en route to the women survivors of Srebrenica.

Of course, we weren't sure the supplies would find them. The women and children might have moved on by then. The workers might not be able to find them again. But with the boxes of underwear went the prayers of many American women.

Six months later, Karen came with me to Bosnia. We found the village and walked into the same community center, where we found the same women and children stuffed into one small room. When we walked in, they all jumped up and embraced us with big smiles. They pulled up the dresses of the girls to show us—they all had clean underwear! We cried, they cried, and we took pictures of us with the women and the boxes of underwear. I remember saying to Karen, "It doesn't get any better than this."

God had called us to find those women, to listen to their pleas, and to respect what they wanted. He helped us get that underwear to the women, not just to provide for them physically but also to offer them hope. He let us be part of a plan so much bigger than we expected that it simply boggled our minds. Providing new underwear might seem like a small thing in a world of pain, but it meant so much to those women—and to us.

"God can do anything, you know—far more than you could ever imagine or guess or request in your wildest dreams! He does it not by pushing us around but by working within us, his Spirit deeply and gently within us"

(Ephesians 3:20–21). If we can only believe this promise and let God work, what a great adventure the second half of our life can be.

3. what really counts

Naomi was an Israelite living in Moab and an undesirable woman in a male-dominated society. She was too old to re-marry, and the sons who were to take care of her in her old age were dead. The property her husband owned had gone to her sons; now that they were gone, neither Naomi nor her daughters-in-law had anything. She was about as low as a woman can go. Some theologians say that Naomi was being punished for leaving Israel in the first place. Maybe. But it wasn't like she had a choice. When her husband, Elimelech, announced that the family was setting out for Moab, I doubt he offered Naomi a vote.

Naomi didn't deserve what happened to her. She seemed to be doing everything she could to live according to the laws of Israel. Her name means "my pleasantness," and the adoration of her two daughters-in-law speaks volumes about the kind of woman she must have been. Every indication points to her relationship with God being ongoing and personal. And for me, also the mother of two sons, it is especially striking that Naomi totally accepted and loved the women chosen by her sons, even though they were not daughters of the covenant and therefore would, on some level, be a shame to her among her relatives back in Judah.

Even though we live in a very different place and time, like Naomi, the path of our lives is often determined by others. We move to follow our husband's job. If we work, we often do so around our children's schedules. We become the caretakers of our parents and the social chairs of our families. Especially in the first half of life, what is important to us is usually what is important to others. We call it being flexible, responsive, caring. We multitask and juggle responsibilities, often without much analysis or perspective. It is easy to get caught in such a reactive frame of mind that we simply keep on reacting even when we begin to have more choices.

MY OWN REACTIONS

The first time I retired, I was forty. I had run my own publishing company for thirteen years and had reached a point where I would either have to make a major investment in growth for the future or limp along at the current level.

Technology had changed everything, and I needed to equip my staff with new systems or we would lose out.

My trusted vice president, Leslie Nunn, who had helped me build the company, had left to be closer to her family. My father had battled a brain tumor for three years and had finally lost the fight. My sons were both in school and had more complex demands than when they were young. My company had been pulled into a lawsuit that had nothing to do with us but cost substantial legal fees to defend our innocence. I was worn out. I wasn't aware of the whisper, but it was already there, calling me to something new.

When a new client asked me to come on board to help acquire a news service and run it part time, it sounded like a great plan. I untangled myself from my own company and walked into what I believed would be a one-year stint as publisher of Religion News Service. One year stretched into five years, mostly because I had such a wonderful situation. My hours were flexible, my job was interesting but not overwhelming, and I was able to pick up my sons from school and attend sports events. It was close to perfect. I had less craziness than running my own company, less travel, and a more predictable schedule. I learned a great deal about the world of newspapers, and I even began to write my own newspaper column. We made great progress with the news service, started a Web service, and increased the revenues. I was able to grow professionally without sacrificing my family time. And I discovered that writing the newspaper column was more enjoyable than I had ever imagined.

I received an award for a series I wrote about Bosnia, and I wrote about experiences from my travels with World Vision and other ministries in Latin America and Africa in my weekly columns. One day, I was on a flight when a man sitting next to me asked what I did. I told him about my publishing job and about my board work with humanitarian organizations. He looked at me and said, "Do you know that your voice changes when you talk about the work you do with the poor? It sounds like that is your real passion. Why aren't you doing that full time?"

This challenge, from a total stranger, made me stop and think. I enjoyed my work at RNS, but I had really accomplished what I had set out to do. The man on the plane was right: I lacked passion for my current work, although it had truly been a great opportunity. It was time to move on. My friend Lorraine had just been diagnosed with breast cancer, and it seemed important to be available to drive her to chemotherapy treatments. It's not so much that she needed me as that I wanted to be with her. And I did want to explore my options in the world of international humanitarian work.

So I retired again. I continued to write my newspaper

column and consulted for some nonprofit clients. I took a
class in fiction writing and tried to write a novel. I left what
I knew and the security of a great job for the vast unknown.
God was teaching me to let go, a lesson I would need to
learn again and again.

A few months later, I was offered a job with a faith-based
humanitarian organization relocating to the area. In my
way of thinking at the time, it seemed like a God-given
opportunity. I was told that it would be a very challenging
job, but I loved challenges. I knew that it represented a
drop in income and a lengthy commute, but it was in the
field I wanted to be in. The job appealed both to my love of
accomplishment and my need to fix anything that was broken. I had developed a reputation as a turnaround person
in the business world. What could be more perfect than
fixing an organization for God? So I launched in, commut-
ing two hours a day to a job that was fascinating and frustrating. For the first time in my career, I did not feel like I
was making progress. The experience I had accumulated
in my business life seemed to have little relevance in this
nonprofit setting. I kept telling myself that if I just worked
a little harder, I could get ahead of the problems. But they
never seemed to end. There weren't enough funds to meet
the needs, and I could barely stay ahead of the crises, let
alone make strategic plans for the future. Nothing I had
done in my career prepared me for the situation I was in.

And personally, I began to be overwhelmed by feelings of frustration and self-doubt. *Maybe I had made a mistake,* I thought. But I was working for a ministry. Surely that meant God had put me there. And besides, I had never been a quitter.

I was sitting in a budget meeting one morning when a secretary rushed in to interrupt our deliberations. "An airplane just struck a building in New York," she said. It was September 11, 2001. By the end of the day, I would learn that a woman I knew had died on one of the airplanes and a parent from my son's school had also been killed. A member of our church died at the Pentagon.

After that day, everything about life in the Washington, D.C., area changed. For months, fighter jets flew over the city, and everyone lived in fear that another terrorist attack would occur soon. The financial problems of our organization worsened, and nothing I tried seemed to work. One day when I visited my doctor, I told him I felt "down." It didn't surprise him. So many people in Washington and New York were feeling down that pharmacies were having a hard time keeping up with the demand for antidepressants. He asked me a couple of questions and handed me a prescription for something he described as a new and very mild drug that would help even out my moods. No, nothing like Prozac, he assured me. I wasn't big on drugs, but I thought I'd give it a try. He had changed my birth-control pills six months before, assuring me that I was too young to be worrying about menopause. I was comforted by his assurances and willing to ascribe my physical and emotional symptoms to the tragedy that had shaken all of us to the core.

What I loved most about the medication was that it made me feel young again. I had more energy and felt more creative than I had in years. I seemed to need less sleep. I was back to my old self again, feeling like I was twenty-five and able to conquer the world. But I was also waking up at 3:00 a.m., unable to sleep and agitated. I felt irritable and frustrated. I was working ridiculously long hours, and even then I was still getting nowhere. I had no time to exercise and had no time for a spiritual life. I lost contact with my closest friends and barely saw my family. I was sinking fast and too proud to admit it.

I began to experience physical problems I could no longer ignore. I was gaining weight and having continuous headaches. In the back of my mind, I wondered if something was terribly wrong with me. *Maybe I was dying.* I finally went to a doctor a friend had recommended who put me through a battery of tests. When we finally sat down to discuss my situation, he was frowning. "Your symptoms aren't that unusual . . ." he began, and in my mind I filled in: ". . . *for a woman who is dying.*"

What he actually said was nearly as bad: ". . . for a woman of your age."

Then he looked at the results of tests my other doctor had taken and compared them to my current tests. "Are you sure these tests were taken just a few months ago?" he asked with concern. I assured him that they had been. "Something is definitely going on," he said. "Have you experienced severe trauma or stress recently?"

I opened my mouth to give my standard line about thriving on stress, but I realized that was no longer true. I just nodded my head.

"Most women go through this kind of change over years. You seem to have compressed it into months. No wonder you are experiencing so many severe symptoms."

I felt both relieved and embarrassed. The doctor wrote a new prescription and with a few scribbles ushered me out of my childbearing years and into hormone replacement therapy. Warning me that it might take some adjusting to get the exact hormone levels correct, he insisted I come back to see him in a couple of months to assess whether it was helping. He had already figured out that I was not going to be a very good patient. And then he told me that I needed to find a way to relieve the stress in my life. "You need to get some regular exercise. And maybe you should find another job," he said.

Taking half of his advice, I joined a gym and started going as soon as the doors opened in the morning so I could still get to the office in plenty of time. I took my new pills and told myself they were working. And I pushed forward with my work, refusing to admit that the job was asking more than I could possibly give.

By the time I came crashing down to earth, I was at the end of my rope physically, mentally, and spiritually. This retirement was a big one. I didn't leave a wonderful success to launch into something even more exciting. When I finally left my job, all I wanted to do was sleep. I felt defeated, depressed, and old. Letting go this time was not so much a freeing experience as a surrender.

BACK ON TRACK

Naomi, as we have seen, had God throughout her trials. I, on the other hand, had only an image of God. I reflected, as I wallowed in self-pity, that God was not acting very godly. I was feeling no justice, mercy, or compassion. I needed him, and he was not delivering. Of course, he was; I just had grown spiritual cataracts. I was ready to have him do *something*, and he wanted me to do *nothing*.

At some point, I dusted off the copy of *The Message* that was sitting next to my bed and began to read it. I was so taken by the beauty of the language that I began to copy some of the Bible verses on index cards. My pile of cards began to grow, and my minutes of Bible reading grew to hours. I found myself clinging to the Word, sucking every morsel out of it. Maybe it was the contemporary language that made the words so fresh. Or maybe it was my total and complete brokenness that gave God a chance at getting to my soul.

I'm not sure I had ever read Lamentations before. But in it I found this passage:

> *"I'll never forget the trouble, the utter lostness,*
> *the taste of ashes, the poison I've swallowed.*
> *I remember it all—oh, how well I remember—*
> *the feeling of hitting the bottom.*
> *But there's one other thing I remember,*
> *And remembering, I keep a grip on hope:*
> *GOD's loyal love couldn't have run out,*
> *his merciful love couldn't have dried up.*
> *They're created new every morning.*
> *How great your faithfulness!*
> *I'm sticking with GOD (I say it over and over).*
> *He's all I've got left. (3:19–24)*

God wanted me. It became more and more clear. He didn't want just a piece of me or just the leftovers. God wanted me to want him more than anything else. He wanted me to understand that if I lived the second half of life like I had lived the first, I would continue to beat my head against the wall. I might have some good days. I might even find another great job, regain my muscle tone, and get back on the treadmill. But that would be small potatoes compared to what he had in mind.

I began to get a glimpse of glory, and I didn't want to settle for less—at least, most days I didn't. I began to keep a journal. It is clear from my entries that I was moving in the right direction, but I was still stuck in some of my old habits. I was still more accustomed to shouts than whispers, and I still felt more of a need to be busy than faithful. Yet I was beginning to see a new road map and attune my ears to a new sound.

I read these words from the apostle Paul: "So here's what I want you to do, God helping you: Take your everyday, ordinary life—your sleeping, eating, going-to-work, and walking-around life—and place it before God as an offering. Embracing what God does for you is the best thing you can do for him. Don't be so well-adjusted to your culture that you fit into it without even thinking. Instead, fix your attention on God. You'll be changed from the inside out" (Romans 12:1–2). I was beginning to see that there was a different way, but I didn't quite know what it looked like.

What will I do? was the nagging question I needed to answer. I was asked to consult for another humanitarian organization, and I agreed, tiptoeing back into the professional world without too much commitment. My father-in-law's health deteriorated, and we began to realize that the end was near. I spent time at his bedside in the last few days of his life, simply trying to let him know that someone was there. I was grateful that my flexible work assignment allowed me to be with him. I began to attend a Bible study, not as an afterthought but as one of the highlights of my week. I read books about health and began to understand more about what had been happening to me physically and how it had affected me mentally.

In my almost comically predictable fashion, I decided to reassess my life and come up with a mission statement. So I went back to the books growing dusty on my shelf. *The Seven Habits of Highly Effective People* by Stephen Covey had helped me set goals earlier in my career.[1] I brushed it off and began to read it all over again. To my surprise, I couldn't remember the book. It seemed to be saying something entirely different than it had before. In light of my new diet of Bible reading, I could no longer view it as a business book. When the book talked about putting "first things first," I no longer saw it as a way of organizing my to-do list. The principle to "be proactive" hit me like a splash of cold water. Being proactive was the opposite of being reactive. Although I might have believed I was being proactive in my life, I was mostly being reactive, which was one of my well-honed bad habits.

I also read Parker Palmer's classic *Let Your Life Speak*.[2] I remembered it to be about vocation, but when I reread it, the words seemed to be saying something else. "Our deepest calling is to grow into our own authentic selfhood, whether or not it conforms to some image of who we ought to be."[3] Taken against the backdrop of Scripture, this quote sounded remarkably like the text from Romans.

My friend Karen suggested that I read *The Path* by Laurie Beth Jones.[4] It, too, seemed to speak about the whole of life, not just work. I walked through her exercises and began to feel like Bilbo Baggins, setting out on an epic adventure I couldn't begin to understand. Somewhere along the line, it occurred to me that I needed to decide what I *wouldn't* do more than what I would do. I made some halting attempts at a mission statement and began to realize that work, as I knew it, was no longer central. When I truly understood this, it was both terrifying and deeply freeing. If I was to get back on the career track, it would have to be a totally different approach. I was no longer trying to build a résumé.

I was just coming up with the final draft of my mission statement when temptation struck. A friend sent me a job notice that seemed "perfect" for me. I read the ad and agreed that the job description seemed to have been written for me. I wasn't ready to launch into such an overwhelming position, but I didn't want to disappoint my friend. I sent my résumé with a cover letter and figured I'd never have to worry about it. But the president of the organization called two days later. He asked me to come in the next week. I was on a roll again. At least I knew enough to pray—really pray. "Make it obvious, please," I asked God, realizing by now that, spiritually speaking, I was at least somewhat impaired.

The location was great. The man was very pleasant. But the job situation was all wrong. I knew it from obvious signs, both small and large. It also occurred to me that I was developing a new way of viewing things. I might have missed most of those signs in the past. I thanked the man for a great conversation but surprised him by declining the job.

One week later, a headhunter called. Several people had recommended me for another job. The organization was well known. The title was impressive. The opportunity sounded really great. Yet, although the organization's purpose was good and worthy, it was not part of my mission statement.

I knew I could do the job, but did I want to spend my time furthering a good cause that was not my true mission? It was a tough decision. I heard the old voice in my head saying, "Don't be a fool." I imagined the big office, the prestigious title, and the sizable income. I tried them all on for a moment, and my heart beat a little faster. But I also heard the whisper clearly now: "Come to me. Trust me. I am all you need." I took a deep breath and declined before I could change my mind.

WHAT SHOULD YOU DO?

By now, you probably realize this is a trick question. Doing is no longer the point. Putting first things first is. I used to be an expert at plotting my future plans. Now I seem to be developing a growing ability to say no. I once planned life in five-year increments. Now I am learning to live fully, completely, and utterly in each day, asking God to make me aware of what he has for me and what I am supposed to see. I still backslide. I still feel anxious at times. I would still rather do than be.

Naomi provides us with a wonderful example of this dilemma. She knew she had to move on, but she had no idea what returning to her homeland would mean. She had left full, and now she was empty. Worse, she had a pagan daughter-in-law who was relying on her. She had no promises and certainly had no inkling of the way God would provide. Even if God had revealed the plot, she would have been aware of all the problems inherent in such a plan. It was impossible, ridiculous, unworkable. And that, I am beginning to see, is just the way God likes it.

I have begun a list in my journal, not of goals but of traits that I would like to develop. So far, my list includes *peaceful, wise, gracious, kind, open, loving, winsome, patient, thoughtful,* and especially *godly.* I have so little understanding of what *godly* really means and so much experience in what it doesn't mean.

My friend Peggy observed, "Being ambitious might have been fine when we were younger, but it's not very attractive in women of our age. It's so much more important to be gracious." These words reveal why Peggy has been a friend for many years, even if I did ignore her for nearly two years while I worked too hard, as she likes to remind me. I am studying the character traits listed in my journal and am trying to learn how to build them in my life.

I have another list that I carry with me to tame my urges to "do." It's an index card with the heading "Perhaps." Now when I get an idea, I write it on the list. The list contains everything from learning Swahili to starting another company. Periodically, I lay that card on the altar, so to speak, and ask God to show me what activities are from him and which ones are my own ambitions. I continue to be amazed by how God is willing to answer when we ask. More and more I am seeing that some of those seemingly good activities would take me away from what might be the best.

Meanwhile, I try to do what I am given with more commitment. I spent so much of the first half of life rushing that I realize how often I did things poorly. I am learning to treat things like making dinner with a certain reverence. It's not that my cooking has substantially improved; it's that I see it less as a task and more as a joy. When my family likes what they are eating, I don't dismiss their compliments as quickly. I am glad they are appreciating it. There is something sacred in these times that I missed before in the rush to move on to something else.

I am only beginning to understand what is really important. God gives me daily manna, and I am learning to be grateful for it. I have many years of addictions and bad habits to break. I don't want to waste any more time running after "the good that is not the best," as Oswald Chambers puts it.[5] I do not want to prove that I can still work as hard or be who I was when I was younger. That woman had her good features, but she was missing some of the most important things in life. If I am pulled back toward those patterns, I will miss what I am called to see. If I turn up the music of busyness, I will miss the whispers of God's call.

Of course, this is not just a lesson for women of a certain age. It is a message for men and women, young and old, who live in a society that values power and prestige. It takes a great deal of energy to resist the forces that propel us forward toward some mythical "golden ring" of success.

One other growing realization is that I did not always understand the nature of passion. I tended to confuse it with the adrenaline high that comes from frenetic activity. I like to be busy, to be needed, to have too much to do. I like to operate in a slightly manic state. For too long, I associated that "high" with passion. But I was wrong. That kind of passion burns out quickly and needs to be replaced. It is not the kind of passion God calls us to, and it is rarely the kind associated with his purpose. Now when I feel pulled into an activity that generates that type of excitement, I know to stop and ask hard questions.

Whenever I have the chance, I try to encourage younger women to live fully in the season they are in. It seems to me that the younger generation has watched women of my age and realized that we made plenty of mistakes. More of them seem to be choosing to do less and do it well. I try to applaud that tendency whenever I see it. "There is plenty of time," I like to tell younger women. "You don't have to do it all."

No matter what our age, we can learn that same lesson. We don't have to do it all; we just have to focus on what really counts.

4. making peace with the past

We know surprisingly little about Naomi's past. For all of the rich detail the Bible gives us about her situation, it seems strange that we would know so few specifics about her husband and sons. We don't know if they died suddenly or from long illnesses. We don't see any evidence of the circumstances causing Naomi to wonder what went wrong or if she could have done something different.

In that absence of information there seems to be a basic principle: Naomi didn't get stuck in the past. She didn't replay the good times or the bad. Chapters aren't devoted to what she might have done differently or how unjust it was that both sons were killed. She doesn't spend time holding a grudge, seeking revenge, or asking what might have been.

If Naomi had dwelled on such thoughts, she might have used up her time and energy getting even. She could

have become critical of her daughters-in-law and angry
with her late husband for bringing her to such a Godfor-
saken land. She might have tried to attract another man
or asked Ruth's family to take her in. She might have done
any of those things, but she didn't.

Naomi was busy looking to God for her second calling.
She didn't name it that or even imagine that God had anything special for her. But one of the most striking aspects of
her story is how much it is rooted in the present and future
and how little it relates to the past.

THE CHALLENGE OF
RELEASING OUR PAST

Giving up the past may be the greatest challenge we face
during our midlife. We want to hold on to so many of the
good things—our looks, our energy, and our roles that once
defined us. We also tend to hold on to the bad as well—the
insults, betrayals, criticisms, and injustices.

On one hand, such tendencies are natural. We can even
justify them by claiming to want to be as good as we
can be. But unless we come to grips with the fact that being all we can be means something entirely different at this
stage of life than it did when we were twenty, we will spend
our days and years trying to become imitations of our former selves. Yes, we should take our health seriously and be
aware that what we eat and how much exercise we get will

have a very real impact on our ability to enjoy future years. But we should do such things not out of vanity or competition but because we want to live a quality life and not be a burden to others. There is nothing sadder than an aging woman living in denial.

We may especially mourn the loss of our children as they grow up and no longer need us. But if we don't let them go and encourage their independence, we are not fulfilling our rightful role in their lives. Many women who were terrific mothers of toddlers and early teens become negligent mothers of nearly adult children. *Negligent* may sound like a strange term, but I have learned that unless we give our children the skills and encouragement they need to leave us and live independently, we are creating an unhealthy dependence in them. If we don't create a new foundation for our relationship, we will miss out on the joy of adult friendships with our own children.

At first I loved that my son Chase would call me from college to ask advice or help him make a decision. But gradually I realized that such phone calls were not necessarily a sign of my success as a mother. I needed to learn to push Chase back toward independence if he was going to be a confident man. I needed to love him so much that I would let him fail on his own and make mistakes. I had to stop holding on to the past closeness I so enjoyed and move to a place that was painful for me but necessary for my son. As much as I loved our relationship as it was, I needed to make a change that might leave us both missing the familiar.

As we have worked at this, Chase and I have developed new patterns of respect for one another. I try to celebrate his decisions even when they aren't necessarily ones I might have made. He has learned to ask for my advice and then feel free to accept or disagree with my opinions. We now have a relationship that is less like the past but is large enough to embrace the future. It isn't always easy for either of us, but we know we are building a solid basis for our future relationship.

My friend Julie had a similar epiphany with her hair. She had worn the same style through most of her adult years, although now she had to cover the gray and work a bit harder to achieve the "natural" look. One day, she walked in to her hair salon and said, "Cut it." She was not only referring to her hair, but also to her ties to the past. She told me that she had looked at her family Christmas pictures and noticed how much everyone else in the family changed, yet she seemed to stay the same—with a few more wrinkles but always the same hairstyle.

It suddenly struck her that she was trying to hold on to "the Julie of Christmas past." She knew exactly how to style the haircut she had and knew that it was still flattering, even after all these years. But there was something about it that was too familiar. Julie's new, natural cut is short, spunky, and gray. It suits her and will certainly stand out in this year's picture. For her, it is symbolic of redefining herself not as someone clinging to the past, but as someone who is fully invested in the present and future.

Leaving good things behind can be hard. But leaving the pain of the past can be far more challenging. To some degree, we all have places in our hearts where the past is still gripping us. The pain of a loss can still bring tears, and the memory of betrayal can tighten our stomachs. We can replay scenes and rewind words over and over again.

The amount of time and energy we spend on the past robs us of time, space, and energy for the future. If you get nothing else out of this book, please, please take this warning seriously. *You must let go of your past.* It won't be easy. You may need help. But wiping the slate clean may be the most important work of this time in your life. If you hold on to past pain, you may spend the rest of your life as a bitter or defeated person. God will only be able to work in a small part of your soul because it will already be full of scar tissue.

THE SLIVERS BENEATH THE SKIN

One day, my Bible study group was listening to a sermon by pastor Tim Keller of Redeemer Presbyterian Church in New York. The sermon was on the topic of envy. At first, I couldn't really think of anyone I envied to the point of sin; nevertheless, I asked God to show me if there was something lurking in a corner of my heart that I was missing.

The name that came to mind was shocking. I couldn't even imagine why I had thought of her. She was a former business associate I had never particularly liked or admired. She seemed to me to have an overblown ego and poor work habits. But as I thought of her, I realized that she had gained the approval of someone I did admire. And there it was: envy. I resented this woman because, in my opinion, she had not "earned" the approval she received. And I resented our boss for not seeing the situation clearly.

That's when I began to get at the root of a deep problem in my life. I was an achiever who often tried to accomplish something in order to win approval. It was a characteristic that had driven me to achieve good grades, work hard for promotions, and even write articles that would win awards. As much as I pretended to be independent and unmoved by awards or honors, I realized how deeply I needed the approval of people I admired and how deeply I hurt when I was overlooked. And if someone received what I considered undeserved approval, I often reacted with resentment.

GETTING TO THE TRUTH

I wrote down this discovery in my journal and began to ask God to purge me of envy, the cancer that had probably colored more relationships than I knew. A few days later, I was praying when the name of a friend came to mind. I hadn't thought of her for years, partially because even remembering her name brought pain. We had been very close, like sisters. I had been willing to do anything for her and had time and time again gone out of my way to support her, encourage her, and help her through tough times.

Then one day, without warning, she turned on me. She shut down, turned away, and didn't even return my telephone calls. It was a perplexing and painful situation. There had been no argument between us, and even our mutual friends were stunned by her coldness to me. I couldn't imagine what I had done wrong or what I might have done differently. All of our mutual friends agreed that her actions were harsh, shocking, and irrational. She wounded me deeply, and I kept thinking she'd eventually come around and apologize. But she never did. Weeks turned into months and months into years. My hope for reconciliation eventually died. Our friendship was simply a memory.

All this time later, the memory was still painful. In his book *Everything Belongs*, Richard Rohr says that God often has a reason for pain, so "we dare not get rid of the pain before we have learned what it has to teach us."[1] While I don't think God wants us stuck in the past, I do think he will show us if there is a reason that, after prayerful petitioning, we can't let something go. I was convinced that this situation was one of those times. So I prayed that God would show me what it was about this situation that still made it so painful. After all, if my friend had irrationally turned on me, why couldn't I just accept that it was her problem and really not about me at all? If that was the case, I had simply loved an irrational, unstable person. I'd done my best to be a good friend, but apparently she had needed more.

During this time, I came across a book called *Loving What Is* by Byron Katie. It's not a Christian book, and I don't agree with many of the things Katie has written and endorsed. But all truth is God's truth, and, in my opinion, the process that Katie outlines in this book is consistent with the Bible. The way the book came to me seemed more than coincidental, so I decided to try a method Katie calls "The Work." [2] As a first step, she suggests that you take a situation that is causing pain and write down all of your thoughts and beliefs about it. She urges you to get downright petty. So with that encouragement, I did. I began to write all my feelings about this person, whom I'll call Mary.

Mary took but rarely gave back. Mary expected me to be there for her, but whenever I needed something she wasn't there for me. Mary used me. Mary expected me to clean up her problems. Mary was not honest with me. Mary borrowed things and never returned them. Mary didn't care how much she hurt me. Mary was never loyal to me. Mary called me late at night and never asked if she was bothering me. . . .

Once I got the hang of it, I was amazed by how my feelings flowed. I did get downright petty. I was surprised by the specifics I could still remember and the anger I felt over all I had done for Mary and how little I deserved her treatment of me. I quickly filled a sheet of paper with my accusations, resentments, and hurts.

What's so Christian about that? you may wonder. I did, too, at first. But this step is such an important part of healing old wounds that I really searched Scripture for understanding. I think this is all part of coming clean with ourselves and God. Certainly, the Lord knows that we are holding on to all these nasty thoughts. Yet we delude ourselves so that we can believe we are good people. Trust me, when I looked at this page of whining and bitterness, I was astounded by how nasty I sounded. And in my mind, I wanted to believe that I was the good and worthy person in the relationship who had been hurt by mean old Mary.

In his book *The Lies We Believe,* psychologist Chris Thurman says, "Most of our emotional struggles, relationship difficulties, and spiritual setbacks are caused by the lies we tell ourselves."[4] These words are so true. Just think about how Jesus dealt with people who came to him for healing.

The woman at the well dodged the truth about her marital status, and Jesus had to confront her with reality before he could heal her. The man at the pool of Bethesda whined about his inability to get to the water until Jesus asked him bluntly, "Do you want to get well?"

Human beings are masters of delusion. Without coming clean, it's hard to find healing. And after living a few decades, most of us have developed a pretty good ability to lie to ourselves. And it was beginning to dawn on me that I hadn't told myself the whole truth about my relationship with Mary.

LETTING GO OF LIES

Truth telling had become an emerging theme in my devotions and prayer time. I had even read that the word *impeccability* means "without sin." So being impeccable with my words meant I would be without sin in what I said. The more I practiced this concept, the more I realized how very casual I was with my words. I was especially struck by the next step in "The Work," which was to go through all the statements and ask, "Is it true?" I had really gotten on a roll, so I had to cross out some of my statements, especially ones that included words like *always* and *never*. For example, statements like *I was always there for Mary* and *Mary never offered to do anything for me* were clearly not the whole truth. I crossed those out.

Then some deeper questions emerged. I had to look at all the statements that included the word *should*. Whenever I found the words *should* or *shouldn't*, I began to see that there was something wrong with my belief. For example, in that statement *Mary shouldn't have asked so much of me*, I began to understand one of the roots of dysfunction in our relationship. Mary could ask whatever she wanted to ask, and I had the right to respond or refuse. The reality was that Mary asked me to help her many times. I was not only happy to do so, but I encouraged her to ask. Our relationship began to be built around her asking and my responding.

Another question from "The Work" is a principle I had already struggled with—one that is a basic tenet of *The Seven Habits of Highly Effective People* by Stephen Covey. The principle, simply put, is this: ask yourself, "Is this my problem or not?" Katie says there are three types of business in the world: mine, yours, and God's. We have to ask, "Whose business is it?" I went through what I had written, and I began to see another big trend. I had decided to make Mary's business and God's business my business. My control tendencies were often lurking beneath the surface.

After going through that round, I was beginning to realize that the statements left standing might be shaky. Katie urges readers to go through the list again, asking, "Can you absolutely know it's true?" If the answer is yes, a helpful exercise is to follow the statement by saying, "Yes, and it means that_____." Suddenly I began to see how I was projecting my own meaning into what I believed to be objective statements. "Mary called me late at night without ever asking if she was bothering me, *and it means that she wasn't considerate of me.*" Wait a minute. Mary was a night owl. Mary didn't wear a watch. Mary was a free spirit who never thought about the time. I was the one who had to get up early. If it bothered me to be called after a certain hour, I should have said something. Or I could have taken the phone off the hook.

Another way to look at these statements is to ask what the proof is that the statement is true. If I were called to testify in a court of law, what evidence could I give for my beliefs about the situation? I know this sounds a bit silly, but I realized that some of my proof was that our friends agreed with me. But did I really ask for their honest opinion, or was I seeking help in soothing my hurt feelings? During the course of my inquiry, I called a mutual friend. "Remember when Mary just stopped talking to me?" I asked her. She hesitated. I pushed. "Don't you remember how all of a sudden she turned on me?"

After a bit of prompting, my friend said, "Well, I don't think it was actually so sudden. I remember she started pulling away, and it was hard for you. Remember how she stopped going to lunch with all of us? I think part of the reason was that she needed a little distance from you."

I felt as if I had been shown a tape of a situation, and the images playing on the screen were completely different than my memory of them. Maybe the breakdown in our friendship hadn't been so sudden. Of course I remember her not going to lunch with the group, but it had never occurred to me that I was the reason. She had said she was too busy. And she had still called me whenever she needed help. But apparently others saw that she was pulling away from me. Worse, when I asked my friends for feedback about the situation, they could tell that I was asking for comfort, not truth.

CHANGING REALITY
AFTER THE FACT

I was seeing the power of my self-deception as I went through this process. There are other steps in Katie's process that may be helpful to some, but the most powerful piece for me was yet to come. After all the testing for truth in "The Work," Katie then suggests a final step, called "The Turnaround." Turning the remaining statements around is an incredibly powerful but very difficult part of the process. I can't do it effectively without much prayer and prompting by the Holy Spirit. So I enter what is called "The Turnaround" only after I have asked the Lord to guide me through it.

Whatever statements remain are now turned around. For example, *Mary wasn't very loyal to me* is turned around to *I wasn't very loyal to Mary*. My immediate reaction to this was denial and even a bit of frustration. Of course I was loyal to Mary. So I prayed, "Lord, show me if there was ever a time I wasn't loyal to Mary." I really meant it, and the Lord answered my prayer. I remembered a time when I had told another friend I couldn't be somewhere because I had to help Mary. Wow. All of a sudden, I realized that I said things like that to make myself look needed. But was that fair to Mary? Wasn't I possibly making her look needy, weak, and vulnerable? It hit me like a ton of bricks. Statement after statement, when I prayed and asked God to show me, turned out to be true of me more than Mary.

All of a sudden, I was faced with an undeniable truth: I was the one who had wronged Mary. I had wanted to feel needed and to appear strong. I had fostered a classic codependent relationship, and she had finally come to the point where she couldn't stand it anymore. Maybe her actions weren't perfect, but I was hardly innocent. In fact, much of the hurt surrounding our relationship suddenly presented itself to me as lies I had told myself.

So I did something I could never have imagined doing

before. Instead of waiting for the apology from Mary that had never come, I wrote a letter to her. I tried to keep it simple and about me. I apologized for times I had encouraged her dependence on me. I confessed disloyalty and dishonesty. I didn't go into great detail, but I did tell her that after all this time, I now realized how much I was responsible for the breakdown of our friendship. I asked for her forgiveness for the things I had done. I told her that I didn't need to hear from her, but if she felt she could forgive me, that would be great.

It would be wonderful if I could tell you that Mary called me and we were reconciled. We weren't. She sent me a brief note thanking me for my letter. Months before, I would have seen the note as one more indication that Mary was being insensitive to me. But I was not hurt by her response. I had done my part to right the situation, and it was as if what was once a festering wound had been cleaned out and was now able to heal. I was now able to move on.

When Mary's name comes up occasionally, it causes me no pain. I can think of her without a sense of open-endedness. I have now learned from the pain, and I hope I have learned to be a better friend in the future. God used that old, open wound to show me some powerful truths about myself. And above all, he showed me that I cannot always be trusted to see myself clearly.

A NEW VIEW OF PAIN

What I learned as I dug out the wound of my old hurt over my friendship with Mary began to take me on a journey that has truly transformed the way I view pain, hurt, and frustration. As I go through the day, I try to stay aware of times when I am bothered by anything that raises what I would call "emotional heat." For me, that means when my stomach tightens in frustration or when I find myself growing critical or reactive to someone. Often I can't understand all the implications at the time, but I try to take that moment and set it aside to pray about. Sometimes I note it in my journal.

One day, I wrote, "Joe really irritated me when he called today and demanded that I get a board report ready by next week."

A few days later, someone commented about Joe, and I found myself thinking negative thoughts about him. There was definitely something about Joe that was bugging me. So I did as I had learned to do: I began to pray about Joe. "Lord, show me why I am having problems with Joe. Show me what he is feeling and thinking so I can understand why he acts the way he does."

That night, I had a dream about fear. Everyone else in the situation knew what was going on, but I didn't. I felt overwhelmingly afraid and insecure about what was going on. I kept asking people to tell me what was happening, but no one would talk to me. The next morning, I woke up feeling unsettled—and then I thought of Joe. Could it be that he was acting out of insecurity rather than self-importance?

The next time I talked to Joe, I decided to think of him that way. When he acted bombastic, I tried to be sympathetic instead of reactive. When he told me he needed something instead of asking me for it, I simply replied that I'd be happy to do it and asked when exactly he wanted it. It was as if I was letting the air out of his tires. By the end of the conversation, his tone had changed and he was confessing his concerns about his job to me. He had been afraid all along, I realized. Instead of butting heads, Joe and I are now allies.

Later, I reflected that part of the reason I had reacted strongly to Joe was that I have the same tendency to make demands on other people when I am stressed. It occurred to me in a moment of holy clarity that the traits that irritate me in others are often the very ones I possess. God was trying to tell me something.

Since then, I have made it a point to try to be aware of any time I am in a situation in which I feel angry, frustrated, critical, or hurt. I know the minute I think, *What's wrong with that person?* God is usually saying it's about me. The sins I see so easily in others are the ones I have become best at ignoring in myself. Now every situation that raises my blood pressure I see as one of God's tools for instructing me.

I don't want to live the rest of my life as a bitter woman. I want to keep cleaning out the spots in my heart that are prone to anger and frustration. I want to move forward to fulfilling the future that God has for me without being weighed down by the pain of the past.

5. leaving the baggage behind

The Book of Ruth tells us that Naomi "went forth out of the place where she was" (Ruth 1:7 KJV). There is something definite about that phrase. Naomi was leaving Moab behind. The biblical record says nothing about her packing up her household or giving away her belongings or agonizing over the memories built in this place. She just got up and left it all behind.

It sounds simple, yet that one phrase strikes me as terribly profound. How, exactly, do we really go forth out of the places where we are stuck? How do we tame a lifelong problem with anger or avoid a tendency to nag or stop being passive when we should act?

In their book *God Will Make a Way*, psychologists Henry Cloud and John Townsend describe a concept called "finishing." According to Drs. Cloud and Townsend, we all have

relationships, experiences, and lessons in life that are sometimes painful, difficult, and, for whatever reason, hard to
process. As a result, we walk around with certain feelings,
patterns, and conflicts that do not relate to the present but
to people and events from a previous time. Because those
things are not "finished," they get in the way of present situations, present relationships, or present goals.[1]

What the authors are describing is something more than
a hurt or bad habit. They are talking about something that
becomes grooved into our lives. The unfinished business
from our childhood or issues that defined us in the first half
of our lives continue almost predictably into the second
half. In many ways, they become more obvious. No longer
young and spunky, we become cranky and crotchety. While
we were once motivated go-getters, we become unstop-
pable steamrollers. What appeared to be a conciliatory
tendency in our youth now looks more like being a dishrag.
We become stripped down to our basic tendencies, and it
isn't always a pretty picture.

God Will Make a Way, along with its corresponding
workbook, is an excellent resource if you feel like you have
some unfinished business in your relationships. I personally
found the book helpful on this topic and many others.

I also discovered another source of help in the powerful
practice of praying the Scriptures. The idea is to take a
scripture and change it into the first person. For example,

I took a verse like Jeremiah 33:3 and turned it into this: "Lord, I know that if I call to you, you will answer and tell me great and unsearchable things I do not know." When I began to fret, I would look at Isaiah 45:2–3 and pray, "Lord, I believe in your promise that you will go before me and make the rough places smooth; you will shatter the doors of bronze and cut through their iron bars. And you will give me the treasures of darkness and hidden wealth of secret places, in order that I may know that it is you, the Lord, the God of Israel, who calls me by name."

There is something amazingly powerful about praying the Scriptures. Somehow I am taken out of my own situation and reminded that the omnipotent God has promised to handle the problems for me. I can pray a verse that King David himself used as he came before the Lord thousands of years ago.

Praying God's Word by Beth Moore is a great resource because verses are already personalized and divided into sections.[2] So if you are struggling with depression, for example, you can go straight to the section on depression to find appropriate verses.

WHEN WE NEED OUTSIDE HELP
Sometimes we need more help than we can find in books. As I tried to purify my heart, I thought of a situation I had been involved in that still perplexed me. I wasn't sure what

had been my fault and what had been simply a bad situation. I wanted to own my problems, but the circumstances were so complex they baffled me. Try as I might, I couldn't see my way through the situation. Something about the issue made me think of the idea of finishing; yet as many times as I reread the section in *God Will Make a Way*, I couldn't find clarity.

One day, I overheard a friend talking about a Christian counselor. I asked her about her experience, and she told me that the counselor had helped her immensely. So I asked for her name.

It took me two weeks to call the counselor. I think I was still too proud to admit I needed help and still confident that I could work it out alone. Like too many Christians, I thought professional counseling was for people with serious problems. I told myself I was normal, just a little bruised by life. And I suppose I also had a sense that even the nagging pain was better than confronting the circumstances again and reliving them. *Get over it*, I told myself. But when I didn't, I finally called for an appointment.

When I met Dr. Moore, I was amazed by how God had put me into a situation where I could feel comfortable and confident in sharing my problem. Dr. Moore was about my age, and I immediately liked her. I could easily think of her as a friend and contemporary. During the next weeks, she patiently and wisely took me through the circumstances of the situation. She wanted to hear everything, and I discovered I was relieved to have someone to tell even the small details. It was often in those small details that she found significance. "Wait a minute," she would say. "Tell me that again." Sometimes in the retelling, I would be surprised by a surge of emotions. I was embarrassed to discover that I was even crying at times over something seemingly silly.

Out of that one painful situation came some of the richest lessons of my life. I began to see how my need for success could lead to anxiety and panic when situations were out of my control. I began to understand that what looked like a sense of responsibility was actually pride and could lead me to "enable" others. I began to see that even though I imagined myself to be independent, I was really a people pleaser who spent a great deal of time seeking the approval of others, even at the expense of myself and my relationship with God. I even learned about some of the ways I was wired and how I should avoid certain situations that would easily hook me into unhelpful behaviors.

Dr. Moore also introduced me to the concept of self-care and helped me understand how my tendency to take care of others could lead me to ignore my own very real needs. Together we adapted the information included on the following page. I've shared this information with dozens of women since then, and almost every one of them finds it to be amazingly eye-opening.

SELF-CARE

Self-care is NOT:

- Taking without concern for others
- Grasping, greedy, mean
- Selfish
- Manipulating others to get attention, care or love

Self-care IS:

- Having concern for others but not at your own expense
- Getting enough sleep, good food, and exercise to remain physically healthy
- Finding mental stimulation to keep mentally alert
- Spending time with people who like and respect you
- Not expecting one person or group to meet all your needs

Self-caring PEOPLE:

- Do for others because they want to; not to get something in return
- Act without fear of what others will think because they get satisfaction from the action itself, not the reaction of others
- Share love and are able to accept love in return
- Are able to care for others because they recognize and find the love and attention they themselves need
- Know they are neither marvelous nor insignificant
- Understand they are important but not indispensable

· Allow others the dignity of making their own mistakes and claiming their own successes

· Accept themselves and others as they really are, with all their faults and strengths[3]

In reviewing my medical history, Dr. Moore connected the significance of my alcoholic grandparents with my experience with the drug prescribed by my gynecologist. I had experienced a pharmacologically predictable manic episode brought on by the combination of prescriptions, stress, and family history. My post-9/11 depression was probably tied to the new birth-control pills I had been on for a few months. The antidote to that put me into overdrive. While most people would have considered that manic feeling negative, I actually felt comfortable being able to work at a crazed pace and saw it as a sign that I was feeling young again. My past addictions to work and achievement had enabled me to embrace the drugs that were helping me feel "superhuman."

I made it a point to learn more about how my family history and how my wiring affected my emotions, my reactions, and my preferences. I was especially intrigued by books written by Dr. Daniel Amen, who had done some cutting-edge research in brain imaging. *Change Your Brain, Change Your Life* taught me that stress, poor diet, and lack of exercise don't just affect my body; they actually affect the way my brain works.[4] I learned that as I aged, there were things I should do to keep my mind sharp and help build resistance to the onset of Alzheimer's. And I began to understand that based on my history, strengths, weaknesses, and preferences, I could come up with a pretty good idea of how my brain was wired.

It was no wonder that I had enjoyed the fast-paced world of marketing and thrived in places where I juggled a variety of tasks. My supercharged frontal lobe loved attacking goals and checking tasks off a to-do list. But it also had a tendency to move in the direction of Attention Deficit Disorder (ADD), making me highly distractible in certain situations. While regular exercise and a high-protein diet could help regulate that tendency, I also learned that prayer and meditation on God's Word was as helpful to my physical and emotional life as it was to my spiritual life.

It was also no surprise that sitting in long meetings made me irritable. As I thought back, I had never been good at sitting still, even as a child. I began to realize that those hourlong church services of my youth did not frustrate me because I didn't love God enough but because God had made my brain in a way that made me a sprinter, not a long-distance runner. I saw that the reason I responded so well the first time I encountered a praise service was that it was fast-paced, auditory, and visual; thus, it hit all my God-created buttons.

I also learned that ADD and other tendencies are highly hereditary. I thought of my seventy-something mother, still running around at a frantic pace, and I had to laugh. She has always done several things at once. Then I thought of my younger son, Tyler, and his tendency to be like me in so many ways. I began to wonder if maybe some of his struggles in school were related to a tendency toward ADD. I made an appointment to have him tested and discovered that he did, in fact, struggle with ADD, although his high IQ and tendency to be a people pleaser had masked it. While I was sorry we had waited so long to diagnose Tyler, I was at least grateful that he wasn't my age before discovering the way his brain was wired.

The book that put it all together for me was Dr. Amen's *Healing the Hardware of Your Soul*.[5] It showed through actual brain scans how a brain could be "cooled down" by prayer and meditation. I'll talk more about what I learned in the chapter on prayer. But for now, let me simply say that the understanding from this book helped me stop trying to fit in to certain spiritual practices that weren't meaningful to me and helped me understand that as a visual learner, for example, I could have a far more vital spiritual life if I didn't fight my God-given wiring.

I had asked Dr. Moore to help me get over a particular situation. But I began to see that God had not erased my memory because he was using it to teach me important lessons about myself. After a few months, I no longer asked God to help me forget the situation; I actually came to the place where I could thank God for it. It's not that the pain had completely gone away. But what I had learned about myself and what God wanted for my future was so much bigger than the pain. Now I knew where some of my unfinished business came from and what I could do to handle it in the future. Looking back, I had to thank God that he had led me through the fire of that situation in order to help purify me for the future.

Perhaps Naomi also had a moment like that as she held baby Obed. God had blessed her with an extraordinary grandchild who would be the grandfather of David and in the lineage of Jesus. She didn't know Obed's significance to the world at that point, but she certainly felt his significance in her own life. Yet without the loss of her husband and sons, she never would have come to that point. God had redeemed her pain and sorrow, and he gave her a place in history she could never have imagined.

THE HELP OF A FRIEND

My friend Linda is one of those homemakers who make cooking, entertaining, and decorating look totally effortless. One day, I was at her house sharing a cup of coffee when she asked me to grab something out of her pantry. I opened the door and literally gasped at the organization.

Everything was in its place and easy to locate. That morning I'd started an avalanche in my own pantry by taking out an item. When I commented on how much I admired her organizational abilities, Linda said, "Next time we have coffee, let's do it at your house. I love to organize, so I'll spend some time on your pantry."

My pride might have gotten the best of me, except that I had learned that my brain wiring was at least part of the reason I was chronically disorganized. Reading a book on organizing for the ADD person had helped me realize that I would be better off having help to get rooms like my kitchen organized. I had thought of hiring a professional organizer, but that seemed like such a waste of money. However, to have Linda helping me would be a pleasure. Besides her ability to organize and run a house, Linda is the most accepting person I have ever known. I have always felt total grace with Linda. She loves me with such openness that I felt like whatever awful things she found growing in my pantry would never lead her to gloat or share the story with a friend.

So one day Linda and her oldest daughter, Kate, home from college, came to visit and set about organizing. They were ruthless at times. Our trash can was overflowing that week. And when they left, my pantry looked almost empty. They had combined half-full bottles and thrown out old spices. My shelves were now so accessible that my whole family would be able to find something if I asked for help. Linda had asked me how often I used certain small appliances that I didn't even remember I had. Out they went. When she found spices and utensils I used often, she moved them to a more convenient spot.

Now that my kitchen is well organized, it is relatively easy for me to keep it neat. But I couldn't have organized it on my own. I needed help, and Linda was the perfect person to get me in shape. Instead of staying stuck in my rut, I found help through a friend.

THE BIGGER PICTURE

Most of us come to midlife with baggage we don't even notice. Have you ever spotted yourself in a window or mirror and wondered who that woman is? Even though most of us look at our faces in a mirror several times a day, we still don't have an accurate picture of who we are. We are probably far more clueless about how others view us and how our mental health affects our reactions. Just as we should have a physical checkup, I highly recommend finding a Christian counselor and having a mental checkup too. What I have learned has truly changed my emotional and spiritual life. It has saved me from repeating mistakes of the past and allowed me to move forward with an understanding of my strengths and weaknesses. It has even helped me help others in a meaningful way.

Come to a place where you can see yourself clearly, and then ask God to help you learn what you can from it. Don't be discouraged by your faults. The sixteenth-century Christian known simply as Fenelon once said this: "Don't be surprised at the defects in good people. God leaves weakness in all of us. In those who are advanced, the weakness is out of proportion to the otherwise mature life." That's a very freeing way not only to judge others more gently but also to look at ourselves.

In another passage of *Everything Belongs*, Richard Rohr reminds us that God is asking us "to be born again and again and again."[6] What he means is that our spiritual lives are not static and that our walk with God is not based on just one moment in time when we give our hearts to God. God is calling and calling us to himself. I am convinced that much of what keeps us from experiencing an exciting future is that we are holding on to the past in a way that is not godly. We are like Gollum in J. R. R. Tolkien's *Lord of the Rings* trilogy, letting memories of "Precious" make us bitter and ugly.

In *When the Heart Waits*, Sue Monk Kidd talks about being at a retreat where everyone was given a piece of paper and told to tear out a shape that represented his or her own life. The shapes were collected and displayed for everyone to see and admire the creative expressions of the participants. Then someone came around with a bowl to collect all of the ripped and torn pieces that remained. Those pieces were taken up to the altar and prayed over as a symbol of the places in lives where tearing had occurred in order to produce the person.[7]

I believe God wants us to hand our torn pieces over to him. Sometimes he will use a piece to teach us something more. But eventually he wants us to move on, confident that what he is calling us *to* will be so much more than anything he is calling us *from*.

6. giving up idols

The Moabites were an interesting group. They had a
great deal in common with the Israelites, except for one
major difference—they didn't worship Israel's God. The
Moabites spoke nearly the same language as their neighbors in Judah, and they knew all about Yahweh. The his-
toric Moabite Stone, an archeological treasure, proves that
they were aware of the God of Israel, yet they worshiped
a god named Chemosh. Looking at the situation from a
few thousand years' perspective, it's easy to see that the
Moabites bet on the wrong horse, so to speak.

But put yourself in Naomi's shoes. She married a nice
Jewish man and bore him two sons. Then a famine hit their
homeland, Judah. In order to provide for his family, Elimelech took his wife and sons to Moab, where, although
the people did not worship Yahweh, they appeared to be
blessed. The Moabites' soil held moisture better, so while

Judah was in the throes of a famine, Moab was doing fine. The Moabite women were beautiful, and from what we are told of Ruth and Orpah, they were kind and loving. At some point, Naomi had to wonder how bad it was to be a Moabite. Their god was supposedly taking pretty good care of his people. And from a purely practical perspective, she must have wondered, *What could Yahweh do that Chemosh couldn't?*

Naomi doesn't seem to waver in her belief in the God of Israel, even after her husband and two sons die, leaving her in the pagan yet apparently abundant land of Moab. If Naomi was a practical woman, she might have added up the tally sheet and figured that her God hadn't done much for her lately. She might have abandoned the belief of her heritage and moved on to that ever-so-accommodating god of the Moabites. Then she might have been able to stay in that fertile land, throw herself on the mercy of her daughters-in-law, and live happily ever after. Practically speaking, that was the thing to do.

But Naomi stayed faithful to her God, despite all the evidence that Chemosh was delivering for the Moabites. Perhaps Naomi's belief was strengthened when her daughter-in-law told her that she was ready to leave not only her land but her god. Ruth had observed Naomi's unwavering faith in Yahweh, and she concluded that Yahweh was worth following even if the evidence didn't exactly add up on his side of the ledger.

Most commentaries don't give the Moabite's god, Chemosh, much attention. He didn't stand the test of time. In the end, he was just one more false idol that was worshiped by people who didn't accept Yahweh, the one true God. The Moabites went down in history as idol worshipers. Despite the relatively peaceful interlude during the Book of Ruth, they were at war with the Israelites much of the time. But during Naomi's lifetime, the Moabites must have seemed to have it made.

Ruth's decision to make Naomi's God her God stands out as one of the great decisions of the Old Testament. It is even more amazing when you realize the circumstances. Ruth turned her back on a god who seemed to be a sure bet in order to follow the God of Israel. Her family must have been shocked, her neighbors perplexed. Naomi was a nice lady, but what did she have to offer? Even she tried to convince her daughters-in-law to go back to their families. She wasn't trying to evangelize them. Naomi knew that it was hard to make a case for following her and her God. There's no way to explain Ruth's decision except as faith. Ruth had come to believe in Yahweh despite what Chemosh seemed to offer.

IDOLS, IDOLS EVERYWHERE

What does all of this have to do with modern-day women? I have come to believe that leaving false idols is at the heart of our ability to hear and obey our second callings.

We're surrounded by idols today. Even if we go to church on Sunday, have a fish bumper sticker on our car, and wear a cross necklace and a WWJD bracelet, we are pretty happy to live among our idols. Most of them are predictable. And practically speaking, they deliver. Worship success, and you often become successful. Obsess about your body by working out all the time, and you will probably have a great physique. Just like Chemosh, in the short term these false idols seem like a pretty good bet.

In his classic book *Addiction and Grace*, the late psychiatrist Dr. Gerald May makes the case that our modern-day addictions are really idols: "Spiritually, addiction is a deep-seated form of idolatry. The objects of our addictions become our false gods. These are what we worship, what we attend to, where we give our time and energy, instead of love. Addiction, then, displaces and supplants God's love as the source and object of our deepest true desire."[1]

Ironically, addictions are "in." We jokingly talk about being addicted to chocolate, Starbucks's coffee, shoes, or any number of things in our daily lives that aren't really such harmless attractions at all. We hardly even notice these addictions unless they are withheld from us or we are jarred out of our normal routine. Idols in our lives are rarely sitting on an obvious pedestal. Instead, they are so entwined in our lives and hearts that we can't even distinguish them. Like the lame man at the pool of Bethesda, we become so comfortable with our condition that we cannot see beyond it. Even when Jesus comes and asks to heal us, we tell him all the reasons that it just wouldn't be possible.

A NEW PERSPECTIVE

As a child, there was nothing I hated more than missions emphasis week at our church. For one week each year, a missionary came to speak every weeknight about his or her life in the jungle or in some far-off land. The dramatic stories merge in my mind: Savage natives. Disgusting food. Terrible conditions. And snakes. There were always snakes, which terrified me more than anything. At the end of a week of these stories, there was always an altar call to ask if anyone wanted to come forward to be a missionary. Even at an early age I wanted to blurt out, "You've got to be kidding!" (My marketing instincts were apparently innate. It seemed to me that a week of horror stories was no way to recruit someone.)

When I grew older, I learned that I loved cities like Paris. But the idea of going to a developing country was still repulsive to me. I couldn't imagine why anyone would want to go to a place that was dirty and where people were poor.

I was no missionary, and never would be. Leave me in my comfortable home and let me earn enough money so I could make generous donations to missions, but don't ask me to actually go there.

A little more than fifteen years ago, I had my first experience in a developing country. After being promised a comfortable hotel and a safe experience, I agreed to go to Guatemala with five other women on what became the first Women of Vision trip. As you can tell from the examples in this book, that trip was not my last to a developing country. It opened my eyes to a totally different way of life and opened my heart to a calling to serve the poor that seems to grow stronger every year.

Years later, when I read Ward Brehm's book *White Man Walking*, I identified with him when he described his first trip to Africa: "My first visit to Africa brought me quickly to my knees. I was out of my element, out of my comfort zone, and it felt terrible. . . . For most of us, our sense of reality and security is based entirely upon the things in our lives that are routine, comfortable, and familiar. Though there is nothing inherently wrong with these things, they can distract us from the need to have our reality and security come from God. Africa forces the issue."[2]

My trip to Guatemala forced the issue for me. I saw many things on that short trip that upended beliefs I had held for my whole life. I met people who had few possessions but seemed happier than most Americans. We visited mothers who loved their children well, despite little education and no assistance from Dr. Spock. I saw poor people who wouldn't think of stealing from their neighbors. I met women who had only one dress and wore no makeup but glowed with beauty.

When I returned home, I saw my whole world differently. Why did I think I needed a closet overflowing with more clothes than I could possibly wear? What was I thinking, living in a house so big when each of the rooms could have comfortably housed a Guatemalan family? Why did our family need so much when so many people in the world had so little? It was a radical and shocking assault on my world-view. And it showed me, for the first time, how much of my life was cluttered with idols.

It's easy to think of idols primarily in terms of possessions. We live in a consumer-driven society and are easily entrapped by materialism. But limiting idols to material things would be too simple and far too obvious. Most of us have idols that are much closer to our identity and much harder for others to see. Romans 1:21–23 shows us how it happens: "People knew God perfectly well, but when they didn't treat him like God, refusing to worship him, they trivialized themselves into silliness and confusion so there was neither sense nor direction left in their lives. They pretended to know it all, but were illiterate regarding life.

They traded the glory of God who holds the whole world in his hands for cheap figurines you can buy at any roadside stand."

In my own life, I can see a correlation between paying lip service to God and running after more and more of the things that gave me quick comfort and instant gratification. I wanted it all, and I made a mad dash in many directions.

I remember watching a television show once in which a person was given ten minutes to grab as much as she could in a grocery store. Everything she grabbed and put in her cart she could keep. It was fun to watch a woman wildly grabbing and throwing items as quickly as she could as she dashed through the store. As I look back at my twenties and thirties, I see my life parodied in that shopping spree. I was grabbing and throwing everything I could into my cart. I wanted a great career, a perfect family, a lovely wardrobe, a practical but sporty car. . . . To come to a place where I must slow down a bit and consider what I'm doing is a gift from God.

We who have reached midlife have been given a holy break, I believe. Most of us have worshiped our fair share of idols. We may not know all their names, but whenever we feel that sense of loss over our looks or figure or youth, we know that we were attached to something. So now we have to choose. Do we trade those in for new idols, or do we get serious about following the one true God? Like Ruth and Orpah, we have to decide whether we will join Naomi on this journey into the unknown or retreat to our old familiar ways.

IDOLS OF THE HEART

A friend sent me the materials from a Bible study on Galatians she was doing in her church in New York, Redeemer Presbyterian. The study, by Tim Keller, was entitled "Idols of the Heart," and I knew when I first started reading the worksheet that it was aimed right at me. I was almost tempted to throw it out because I knew if I read it and took it seriously I would have to change my life.

Part of the worksheet contained a list of the types of idolatry many modern-day men and women embrace. In part, it included statements like this:

> *Approval idolatry:* "Life only has meaning/ I only have worth if I am loved and respected by _____."
>
> *Control idolatry:* "Life only has meaning/I only have worth if I am able to get mastery over my life in the area of _____."
>
> *Helping idolatry:* "Life only has meaning/I only have worth if people are dependent on me."

Work idolatry: "Life only has meaning/I only have worth if I am highly productive and get a lot done."

Achievement idolatry: "Life only has meaning/ I only have worth if I am being recognized for my accomplishments/excelling in my career."

The list goes on, and I could think of a few of my own to add. When we begin to get at the roots of our idols and addictions, it's not a pretty picture. One suggestion from the study is to think about what you fear the most or what you worry about most often. If you follow that trail, you almost always arrive at the foot of an idol.

Do you fear being embarrassed? Are you worried no one will need you? Do you dread losing your physical attractiveness? If so, the idols of pride, helping, and beauty are lurking in your heart. If you have a hard time spotting them, begin to pray and ask God to reveal them to you. I can assure you, from personal experience, that God is very willing to help us open our eyes and see our idols.

One of my idols is busyness. I like that people think of me as busy. It feeds my sense of being important, productive, and on the move. It also serves as a good excuse to get me out of things I don't want to do. Instead of telling someone that I really don't feel called to serve on a committee, I can simply haul out my idol of busyness. I've become very adept at whipping up a dust storm of activities and appearing to be a woman without a minute to spare.

One of the lessons God is teaching me is to be open and not overcommitted. Along with that comes the ability to say, "Yes, I have the time to listen" and, "No, I'm not too busy to be asked." Neither is a comfortable phrase for me. I sometimes end up spending time on things that perplex me. I sometimes have to say no to things for more honest reasons than busyness.

I now often tell people I can't give them an answer until I pray and ask God to show me what I should do. In my younger days, people who told me they would "pray about" simple things irritated me. I thought of them as wimpy and indecisive. Now others may think the same of me. The fact is, I know now that I'm not very good at making my own decisions. The idols still attract me. I have years of idol worship to overcome, and I am very, very good at deceiving myself and falling back into my old patterns.

IDOLS IN DISGUISE

A woman I know, whom I'll call Sandra, is a relatively new Christian. Five years ago, she attended a conference with a friend. For the first time in her life, she really heard about Jesus and decided to follow him. Sandra's husband, a very prominent businessman, wants nothing to do with Sandra's newfound faith. He loves her, but he refuses to go to church with her and asks that she not talk to him about "religious stuff." Although her husband's behavior grieves her, Sandra has prayed and studied Scripture and talked to pastors, and she believes she should just love her husband and not try to evangelize him with words. Still, everything about Sandra's outlook has changed.

When I saw her recently, she was, as usual, dressed impeccably in a designer suit. It was a particularly beautiful shade of blue, and I complimented her on it. She smiled and, with a twinkle in her eye, thanked me. I knew her well enough to ask what was going on, and she shared her secret with me.

It seems that after she became a Christian, Sandra felt unsettled about the wealth of her family and especially her own wardrobe. She was known as a fashion trendsetter, and she often traveled to New York and Paris in order to purchase her next season's wardrobe. Her husband enjoyed the fact that his wife was always beautifully dressed and felt it helped him appear powerful and successful. He gave her a monthly budget for clothing that most women would never spend in a year.

She couldn't exactly take up wearing sackcloth, and she knew she couldn't embarrass her husband publicly. So she prayed and asked God to help her be creative. Meanwhile, she stopped shopping. While her friends went to Fashion Week in New York, she stayed home. "I just kept wearing the same clothes I had the year before and prayed no one would notice," she told me. And while that would mean little to most women, Sandra lived in a social scene where everyone wore the latest fashions. Meanwhile, she took her clothing allowance and began to support a local ministry.

Whenever there was a special event, she would reach to the back of her closet to find a gown she hadn't worn in a year or two. She learned to cycle her suits the same way. The one she was currently wearing was five years old, and she was delighted to tell me how she had taken it to a local tailor and asked him to make a few alterations. "I know this sounds strange, but I feel like the Lord has protected me. Neither my husband nor my friends have noticed that I haven't bought any new clothes in five years."

It might sound strange to praise a woman for wearing a designer suit, but in this case, Sandra has broken her idolatry of being fashionable and avoided becoming self-righteous about it. She had prayed for God's protection so her suddenly frugal ways would not be made into a display. She even had asked God to keep her husband and friends from noticing that she was no longer worshiping at the altar of high fashion. Now she looks back and laughs. "All that time I spent getting the latest clothes and thinking it was so important . . . It just shows how blind we can be!"

While I have to admit that I don't totally identify with Sandra, her example did make me examine my own shopping patterns. Too often I stop at my local Target for a necessity and find myself looking at the cute tops or the trendy shoes. If I'm not careful, I can easily end up with a cart full of fun little things that add up to a surprising amount of money. It's not that shopping is wrong, but I can be just as guilty as Sandra—although I'm operating at the other end of the retail continuum—because I love getting a "deal." I can buy something I don't really need because the price is just too good to resist. Or if one T-shirt is a great deal, I buy one or two more even if I don't really need them. I have to resist "recreational shopping" at times, or at least examine my motives, to keep me from falling prey to the idol of great deals.

IN THE DUMP

You don't have to be wealthy to have idols. I learned this on my trip to Guatemala. One of the most difficult parts of the trip was our visit to the dump just outside Guatemala City. You can smell it before you can even see the massive pile of garbage. It reeks like nothing I have ever smelled before. The mountain of waste includes chemicals dumped from manufacturers, medical refuse from hospitals, decaying food, and even human waste.

As our van neared the seething pile of decay, we were surprised to see movement on the side of the mountain. As we came closer, we were horrified to realize that there were men, women, and children crawling over the garbage, picking through it for food to eat and any bit of trash they could sell. Some of these people, we learned, even lived on the pile of garbage, burrowing in for the night and forming shelter out of decaying and polluted materials.

What broke our hearts most were the children, some still infants, crawling around used syringes and waste without any sense of danger. Since we were visiting with World Vision, we wanted to know why the workers weren't doing more to help these children. Why couldn't we just rescue the children from disease and death and place them in a safer facility?

Patiently, the World Vision workers explained that children who are taken out of the dump and given clean clothes, a place to sleep, and a school to attend often ran away. Time and time again, they tried to rescue the children—and time and time again, they ran right back to the dump. Eventually, they built a school next to the dump. Most of the children ignored it, but the World Vision workers had learned to wait for the children or parents who decided to change their situation and ask about the school. It was hard for us to believe anyone preferred life in the dump over a clean bed and warm food, but we were assured by everyone we met that many people chose to live in that dump.

Later, after reflecting on this, I realized how much all of us are like those people. We are attached to what is familiar. We have learned to love the smell of the dumps in our lives, and we are comfortable living in garbage. We are wallowing in such a cesspool that we cannot see the better life God is offering us. Sometimes we are stuck in a relationship that is familiar but destructive. Sometimes we repeat bad habits over and over, not even wanting to let God take them away. What looks like a dump to someone else has become our home.

THE IDOL OF STATUS

When I was crisscrossing the country almost weekly, I amassed an astounding number of airline miles and began worshiping the idol of status. Eventually I was in the top tier on both American and United Airlines, earning free upgrades on nearly every trip. I hardly ever flew coach for years. Along with that privilege, I acquired the ability to "move to the head of the line" in the world of upgrades.

I recall walking up to the United counter in Los Angeles one day close to departure time and handing over my ticket as well as my shiny frequent-flier card. A few businessmen were hovering at the counter waiting to find out if they had been cleared into first class. They were older and clearly thought it was ludicrous when I asked to see if I could possibly upgrade. "Forget about it," one guy laughed. "I've been on the list for two hours, and they've been turning people away."

When I was handed my boarding pass and told I had just been given the last first-class seat, I thought one of the men would explode. "But she just got here!" he practically yelled at the gate agent. Then he started to tell the agent about how he had been bumped from his last flight and he had work to do on the plane and the only seats left in coach were center seats . . . I almost thought he would cry.

To say I felt sympathetic would be a lie. I was gloating. I loved that special card and the status it gave me. No matter what anyone else thought of me, United Airlines knew that I deserved to be treated like a queen. Of course, all it really meant was that I had been stupid enough to waste half my life flying around the country. But that card was about as close to a graven image as I have ever had. It had the power to bring grown men practically to tears. With my super-duper premier executive platinum card, I ruled.

Eventually I stopped flying so much, and other frequent fliers overtook me. United Airlines did a very smart thing. They announced that since I had flown a million miles on their airline, I would forever more be a "United Million Miler." It says so right on my frequent-flier card. It gives me no benefits except early boarding, which I will soon be eligible for based on age, and an occasional special mailer offering to sell me something. From time to time, an airline employee looks at my card and thanks me for being such a loyal customer. I look at it and remember how silly I was to love a card that got me a slightly larger seat on a big tube hurtling through the sky. That's how idols are. Once they lose their grip on us, they look so silly. But when they have us in their grip, there's no telling what we would do for our idols.

I can laugh at my love of my status airline card, but other idols are more painful. I am still an achiever in recovery. Every day I have worked on this book, I have had to pray that God will do what he wants with it, even if it is to teach me humility. The achiever idol whispers in my ear, trying to make me anxious about how many copies will sell and what critics will think. It's easy for me to get sucked into that trap and worry more about results than obedience.

The important idol urges me to tell people that I'm too busy to do anything else because I'm writing a book. The fact is that I've had plenty of time to write and still do other things; I've just left too much for the end. I'm not too busy or important; I've managed my time poorly. There's little importance or drama in that admission and far more truth.

Some days, I disappoint these idols. Other days, I fall right back into their traps. Some idols lay in the trash heap, never to be missed. But there are idols always lurking around the perimeter of my life, begging me to remember the feeling of being important, being appreciated, being admired. These idols will probably not end up on the trash heap. The best I can do is to fence them out and fill my life with something else. Only God can keep these idols at bay.

It will never be enough to discipline myself to stay away from these idols. Only a growing and vibrant relationship with the true God can help me fill up those spaces once filled by their false promises. Only by knowing God more fully can I see the worthlessness of these idols that tempt me. And even then I know that there will be times when I am vulnerable, when I am tempted to ask the Lord to give me a happy ending or the respect I still think I deserve. *Make me feel like a queen again*, I want to pray.

I have reread *Inside Out* by Larry Crabb so many times that highlighted passages and underlines appear on almost every page. On some well-worn pages I have resorted to stars in the margins to remind myself. One of my favorite quotes is this: "To be changed from the inside out means to learn how to drink from the living water of God's unchanging love so our purpose, identity, and joy give us courage to respond well whether our life is smooth or rocky."[3] I want to be so secure in God that I can see the tarnish around the edges of my idols clearly.

Had I been Ruth, newly arrived in a strange land where I was now expected to beg for my supper, I might have begun to think back fondly about old Chemosh or I might have told the Lord how much I believed in him and how I knew he could show up that old Moabite God. I might have tried to help him be God, because I'm an achiever and easily fall prey to thinking God could use a bit of my help.

But Ruth did none of those things. She was simply and humbly obedient to a God who had given her no special signs. She never looked back, and she only looked far enough forward to see where God was directing her. She fully and completely embraced the power of the living God, and Chemosh couldn't hold a candle to him.

7. a new identity

The rice fields shimmered on the plateau below us, seeming to float on a layer of fog that was rising up from the valley. We stood on a mountaintop, high above an area of northern Thailand that had just taken us the better part of a day to reach. Barely visible was the road—really more of a mud path—that seemed to hang on the very edge of cliffs below us. Hours of coaxing a four-wheel-drive vehicle through deep mud ruts and across deceptively fast-moving streams ended when we simply couldn't make the vehicle go any farther. We had bailed out, thrown on our backpacks, and begun the hike up the rest of the mountain.

Sean Litton, the head of the International Justice Mission (IJM) office in Thailand, offered to carry my backpack. Twenty years younger and an experienced outdoorsman, Sean must have been thinking I would never make it. I was thinking, *I'll keep up or die trying.* I didn't want to be known as the older lady board member who held up the whole group.

Fortunately, I was able to keep up with the group even as the air thinned and the trail turned steep and slick. My reward was an incredible view unlike anything I had experienced before. We were far away from anything I had ever seen in a tiny village of the Karen tribe, hill tribe people who occupy much of northern Thailand. As a member of the board of IJM, I had come to see the work firsthand. In this village, we would be observing a process that would change everything about the future for these people. We would be helping them gain official identities.

Although the people in this village had lived here for generations, they had no official identity as citizens of Thailand. Their ancestors had come from China or Burma and settled in these mountains. For the most part, they were ignored and left to farm the land that no one else wanted.

Then the growing industry of sex traffickers discovered the beautiful children and young women of the hill tribes. They convinced some of them to come to Bangkok to make money working in restaurants so that their families could have a better life. Sadly, most of them found their jobs were not in restaurants but in brothels. When they ran away from these terrible situations, they were faced with another shocking discovery: without any official papers to identify them, the police could do little to protect them. So IJM's work in the Karen village was to warn the villagers of these false promises and to provide people with identity papers, giving them access to government services and making them far less attractive to sex traffickers and others who might take advantage of them.

Most of the villagers had no documents to prove who they were—no birth certificates, diplomas, or licenses of any kind. They knew who they were, of course, but they'd never had to prove it to the rest of the world. Few could read or write. So as we observed the painstaking process of recording information, photographing families, and developing family trees, it became obvious to us Americans that those cards that bulged in our wallets were more precious than we had ever imagined. They gave us instant credibility and identity as citizens, taxpayers, even frequent fliers. Our identities protected us.

IDENTITY CRISIS

During the first half of my life, I accumulated many identities. I was a daughter, student, driver, employee, taxpayer, wife, and mother. A box under our bed holds our family's passports, marriage license, diplomas, and other important documents proving who I am. I invested a great deal in some of my identities. I am still Tyler and Chase's mom, but fewer and fewer people identify me that way anymore. I still have a press pass, although I rarely use it; several frequent-flier cards; and a driver's license with a photo of a much younger woman. I am affiliated with a couple of organizations that have given me business cards, but I prefer to hand out a card with just my name, address, and e-mail. My identity is no longer tied to a title or an organization, although for many years such cards were terribly important to me. If I cared to, I could certainly spin a good story when people ask what I'm doing nowadays; but most times, I don't bother. "I'm doing a bit of this and that," I reply. I've abandoned the ten-second power speech I once had ready to impress anyone who asked.

I'm not alone in this seeming loss of identity. My friend Nancy, a powerbroker in Washington for many years, eventually decided to sell her marketing firm. The work was still exciting, but she wanted to turn her attention to different things. When we met one morning for coffee, she gave me her new e-mail address. I looked at the initials and asked her what the "NI" in her address represented. "New Identity," she replied with a wry smile. "That's not what I tell everyone, but you would understand. I'm no longer known as the president of my firm; I no longer have people being nice to me because of my position on the Board of Trade. My children are adults, and I am now challenged to find my new identity. It's exhilarating and terrifying at the same time."

Nancy and I have shared many a cup of coffee since that day, talking about the new things we are trying that we might never have had time for in the past. She's taken her creative eye that made her so good in a visual business and developed a thriving cottage industry creating ceramic mosaics that incorporate antique porcelain into contemporary works of art. She's moved from being a too-busy-to-attend-every-meeting board member to an active and pivotal chairperson of the same board. She has joined a Bible study and taken a trip overseas with a charitable organization. She has tried many new things, none of which makes newspaper headlines or creates a power base.

This is one of the particularly interesting aspects of this phase of life for many women. Power and fame have lost their appeal. Even women who enjoyed dizzying success in their younger years approach the second half of life with almost a shrug at all that pomp and circumstance.

My friend Betsy was always the "supervolunteer." While her sons were in school, she chaired the Mothers' Executive Committee, ran the school fund-raiser and festival, served on the board, and did just about anything needing organization, leadership, and grace. At church, she was in charge of the women's programs, organizing regular events

SHHH with the ease of a well-run machine. When the church decided to start a Christian school, Betsy was drafted to chair the board and help lead the efforts to find a location, teachers, curriculum, and principal. No one else could imagine taking on such a daunting task. But everyone knew that Betsy was the perfect person to handle it. In her free time, Betsy led a Bible study for her neighborhood and was often a discussion-group leader for a Community Bible Study group.

When we had lunch recently, Betsy confessed that she had stopped attending CBS for the first time in twenty years, had given up her board position, and was pulling back from many of the leadership positions she had held. "I know this sounds strange, but I want to spend more time being available to encourage my friends as well as driving some of the elderly ladies in the church to their doctor's appointments or taking them to lunch and making sure they are feeling cared for." Having lost her own mother in the last year, Betsy realizes how much she loves the company of older women and how much she values serving them.

There's no title to go along with Betsy's newfound priorities, nor is there an easy answer when someone asks, "So what are you up to these days?" But Betsy has already organized and led so many things; now she is called to do something that is almost anonymous. She wants to help each of the elderly women in her church feel loved and cared for in a special way. I doubt Betsy will be any less busy or approach the task with any less enthusiasm than she has done any of her other jobs. Yet as we talked, she asked if I thought it was strange that she had less ambition than she had before.

I told Betsy what I had come to realize about myself and the other women I had interviewed for this book. It's not a loss of ambition; it's a willingness to find a new identity and to let that identity be defined by a holy calling rather than what other people believe you should be doing. What strikes me is how counterintuitive this sense is. Few decisions made in our second stage of life represent a natural progression toward what has been built in the first half of life. It's as if we have to completely turn our backs on our first-half identities in order to invest fully in our second callings.

BEYOND THE IMAGINABLE

Of course, not every woman gets to choose. A friend I'll call Kay was living the life she had dreamed of as a little girl. She and Dan had been married twenty years. They weren't perfect years, but they were good years, with four children, a nice house, two cars, and a dog. She and her husband were members of a large church where they sat in the same pew every Sunday. Dan had moved up the ladder in a business where he had recently been made a vice president. With their oldest two children in college and Dan traveling more often now on business, Kay was beginning to feel she had a little space to breathe. She joined a Bible study, signed up for quilting lessons, and prepared to enjoy the future.

She noticed that Dan seemed a bit more irritable, but she concluded that his new job was more stressful and her life was now less so. Maybe she just noticed his moods more now that she had more time to think. When Dan announced that he was joining a gym in order to get in shape, she encouraged him, thinking it would help him reduce his stress. After losing twenty-five pounds, Dan needed to buy new clothes. Then he got a new hairstyle. And then one day he told Kay what almost everyone else who knew them had suspected: he was leaving.

One year later, Dan married his much-younger secretary and started a new family. Kay was still in shock. She hadn't worked outside the home since she became pregnant with their first child, and she had no marketable skills. Dan had been paying for much of the family's expenses, but he had a new family to support. Kay had to sell the home they had lived in for years and move to a neighborhood where she knew no one. She felt humiliated, betrayed, and desperate. And suddenly she had to find a job in a market where

everyone viewed her as older and without the basic computer skills or job history most companies expected.

Kay was bitter for a while. None of us could blame her.
But then she pulled herself together, earned a teaching
credential, and went to work as a substitute teacher. "I
would never have had the patience or desire to do this
job when I was younger," she told me one day. "But now I
try to come to school and use my mothering skills to make
each child feel special and to make sure the students don't
get behind in their classwork while their regular teacher is
gone." In the meantime, Kay is taking a computer training
class. In her late forties, Kay has a career for the first time.
"I'm different from most of the other teachers. I'm twice
the age of many and without all that impatience of youth.
When they get upset about some change the administra-
tion is proposing, I can just smile and encourage them to
give it a chance. When they have a 'problem child' in their
class, I advise them to try a little more love and attention."

Kay's identity was, for a time, as a divorcée, the woman
who had been dumped by Dan. Kay would be the first
to admit that she wallowed in that identity for a while.
But eventually she got tired of seeing the look of pity on
people's faces. "The first time someone at church told me
that her child said I was a 'cool' substitute teacher, I saw
a sense of respect in that person's eyes. I liked it," she told

me. "This may not be the greatest career in the world, but I want to put everything I can into it. Funny thing is, if I had done this when I was younger, I might not have given it my all. Now I see every day as a chance to show God's love to some child who feels unloved. I see it as a much bigger deal than I would have imagined."

SHIFTING FOCUS

Naomi, as we have learned, was so shaken in her identity as a grieving widow that she told her old friends to call her by a new name: Mara, which means "bitter." Naomi had been "my pleasantness" in the first half of her life when she was fulfilling her call as a wife and mother. But now she had nothing. Her identities were gone, and she saw little hope for the future. She was returning to her homeland without anything—no husband or sons, no income, and no grandchildren. Ruth's devotion to Naomi stood out because, without her, Naomi was alone and without any hope for the future.

My own mother can relate to Naomi's experience. She followed my father to California, away from her Midwestern family and roots, when she was in her late forties. As a young man, my father was stationed at the Marine Corps base at Camp Pendleton and always dreamed of returning to California. When he was offered a job in Los Angeles, he was thrilled. I was already living in Washington, D.C., when my parents packed up and moved to the other coast.

My parents' marriage was traditional. He worked; she cared for the home. My father was always the driving force in decisions, not in a dictatorial way but because he was such a powerful force in our family. If he had an idea, we always went along with him. If he didn't feel like doing something, we usually passed on it too. It just wouldn't be fun if Dad didn't come along. One of his loves was his involvement in Rotary Clubs, where he had often held a leadership role. So when my parents and younger sister moved to California, he joined the local Rotary Club.

Eventually, my father left the company and started his own business as a manufacturer's representative. He reasoned that he was nearing retirement and would be able to continue this work when he and my mom moved to the retirement house they had purchased in the Sierra Nevada Mountains. My mom helped with the business, but, as usual, it was Dad's. Then everything changed. Dad was diagnosed with a malignant and aggressive brain tumor, and he went from being in excellent health to being hospitalized. My mom, who had always been taken care of by her husband, was suddenly faced with taking care of him. And in order to keep his health insurance and to avoid financial losses, she had to keep the business going.

For a while, my father underwent aggressive treatments that left him physically exhausted but mentally aware. My mom would care for him and then, with his direction, take care of business. She had to learn to place and fill orders for industrial materials, package containers, and even operate a small forklift. And she took him, as often as was physically possible, to his beloved Rotary Club meetings.

Mom cared for Dad as long as she could, but my father was a big man, and she couldn't lift him or help him if he fell. After a few calls to the paramedics, we knew we had to find a place for Dad to receive adequate care. So in late November 1993, we placed him in a convalescent home. Mom spent her days there, leaving Dad's side only to keep the business running and to attend Rotary meetings so that the membership stayed active. She knew how much it meant to my dad.

On New Year's Eve, Dad passed away, just a few weeks short of his sixty-fifth birthday, a retirement he had been planning for several years. Yet he'd never planned on having a brain tumor or leaving my mother to fend for herself, far away from her birth family, her Midwestern friends, or her daughters.

Most of us assumed Mom would move back to the Midwest to be near her siblings and friends. But someone gave her the good advice that she shouldn't make any big changes for a year. So she stayed put. She continued going to Rotary Club meetings, mostly because it meant so much to my dad. She even continued to go back to the convalescent home to visit some of the other patients and to volunteer to help at benefits. My father had been treated well there, and she wanted to help support the facility. For a year or two, whenever she did something, she talked about it in terms of what my dad would want her to do.

Then Mom surprised us all—and, as she often says, she even surprised herself. Her lifelong hobby of snapping photos meant that whenever she attended Rotary Club events, she took pictures and then handed them out. Someone asked her to be the official Rotary Club photographer. Her outgoing nature made her a natural to be a greeter at the weekly breakfast meetings, being the first to arrive and welcoming visitors. The club president asked her to serve as the representative to some regional meetings. A local newspaper reporter wrote a story about her when she became involved in the local chamber of commerce. She was no longer identified as the wife of Allan Hanson, a title she had used for much of her life. She was now Irene Hanson, the energetic community volunteer.

When I called Mom recently to tell her I was coming to California and wanted to stop by, she asked me exactly when I would arrive. When she told me all the events she had scheduled, I wondered if she could fit me in. Now in her seventies, Mom has never been busier. And despite missing my father, I don't think she's ever been happier. She has a diverse group of friends who love her for who she is, not for whose wife she is. Twelve years ago, she thought she had lost her world. Now she has an entirely new world.

DREAMS FOR THE FUTURE

I was the thirty-six-year-old senior editor of *Today's Christian Woman* magazine when I interviewed Jill Briscoe for a cover story. A well-known author and speaker, her husband, Stuart, was also the pastor of the burgeoning Elmbrook Church in Brookfield, Wisconsin, and the host of a daily radio show.

I came to the interview surprised to find the normally upbeat and vibrant Jill a bit more reflective and even a bit down. She looked to me like she was just hitting her stride, still writing and speaking, adding some Christian educational toys to her portfolio of accomplishments. But she had recently turned fifty, and she had been surprised by the impact of that birthday on her outlook.

"I don't do a lot of reflecting," she told me, "but I think my fiftieth birthday was very significant. I never expected it to be. I guess it was the sudden realization that I was in the last third of my life. I had never really faced that before. Then on the heels of that comes the reality that I will never do this or that. Up to then I had been saying things like, 'When I grow up I want to be . . .' or, 'Maybe I'll have a go at this . . .' or, 'I will go to seminary one day and finish that degree.' Suddenly I thought, *Ninety-nine percent of those things I'll never do.*"[1]

I asked Jill if she had any regrets, and she said, no, just realizations. "One was that I would never be a full-time missionary. . . . I always had the feeling that maybe we were to stay in the church for a while and then go to Africa. When I became fifty, I realized that I would never do that.

"I also realized that I'll never translate the Bible. I always wanted to go to a tribe, live there for twenty years, and end up with a book in my hand that God had helped me translate."[2]

When I caught up with Jill fourteen years later, I was approaching my own fiftieth birthday with a bit of fear and trepidation. I reminded her of that interview, and she laughed. "Well, it wasn't exactly the end after all, was it?" she said in her British accent with her usual sense of humor. Since I had last seen Jill, she had started a magazine, written a few more books, and traveled hundreds of thousands of miles. She and her husband, Stuart, are on a whirlwind tour of the world, preaching at conferences and encouraging ministry couples in all ends of the world. In any given month, she is in Africa or Asia, keeping a schedule that would exhaust most thirty-year-olds.

Jill has a few more wrinkles, and her hair has gone naturally gray. But she almost looks younger now than she did when I interviewed her fourteen years before. She spends less time in the spotlight and more time being a missionary to those in Africa and other parts of the world. In many ways, she is living the dream she thought she'd abandoned.

I didn't ask her, but I doubt Jill feels "grown up" even now. My guess is that she has many more dreams and will be keeping up the pace as long as she can move. She and Stuart tease each other as if they are dating, and those who work at Elmbrook Church just shake their heads at the schedule they keep.

"We arrive in this world with birthright gifts—then we spend the first half of our lives abandoning them or letting others disabuse us of them," Parker Palmer says in *Let Your Life Speak*. "We are disabused of original giftedness in the first half of our lives. Then—if we are awake, aware, and able to admit our loss—we spend the second half trying to recover and reclaim the gift we once possessed."[3]

I love the idea that we have to turn our backs on some of those identities from the first half of life in order to move toward something more authentic in the second. It's not so much that we are losing our identities, but rather that we are no longer embracing false identities. If we hold on to what once defined us, we will miss out on the authentic identity we are being called to.

In some ways, this is exactly what happened to Naomi. She came back to her homeland, to the place she belonged. Boaz was her relative by marriage, described in that day as her kinsman redeemer. Through his marriage to Ruth, he redeemed both women and gave Naomi her true identity, one she would never have had without God's miraculous intervention. Naomi might have dreamed of being a grandmother when her sons grew up and married, but she would never have imagined she would have this identity after they died.

And although Naomi would never have fathomed it, thousands of years later, her humble life is influencing women around the world, not because of anything she did in the first half of her life but because of how God chose to use her in the second half. We learn from Naomi's example, not because she was an incredible mother or great hostess, but because when she came to the end of herself, she turned to God. He gave her an identity that went beyond anything she might have imagined for herself.

8. without a prayer

From the beginning to end of the short Book of Ruth, everything in Naomi's life changes. Her identity, home, economic status, and even her name go through major upheavals in a few chapters. But one thing remains constant for Naomi—her relationship with God. She never stops talking to him, even when she believes he has completely ruined her life. Even at her darkest moment, she is in regular communication with God.

For those of us who may feel upended by aging, changes in our lives, and fear about the future, Naomi serves as a great example and offers a simple but profound cure for our insecurities. The foundation of our second calling is prayer. This is a calling in itself, as well as the way in which we will find our path through the second half of life. Prayer is a nonnegotiable, and it must take on new meaning and a new role in our lives if are going to live with passion and purpose.

Signa Bodishbaugh, in her classic book *The Journey to Wholeness in Christ*, writes of keeping a prayer journal for twenty-five years. "What a pattern of my spiritual growth I can see as I look back over 25 years! God was calling me to be a woman whom I did not yet know. Although I am still very much a person in process, it is good to know that I am becoming the woman He created me to be, moving down His road toward wholeness. . . . Learning to hear God's voice began to define for me the person He created me to be."[1]

What a wonderful example and challenge as we move forward into the uncharted territory of the second half of life. I love the exciting promise that God is defining for me "the person He created me to be," as someone who is no longer defined by her children or career or many of the things that gave me title and context in the first half of life.

A JOURNEY TOWARD PRAYER

At this point, a confession is in order: I am learning to pray. Yes, I prayed from the time I was old enough to say, "Now I lay me down to sleep." I know how to pray aloud and can give a reasonable public blessing. I have prayed as I begged God to save a life or deliver a teenager home safely. I recite the Lord's Prayer most Sundays and read a confessional prayer in unison with the rest of my congregation. Sure, I can pray with the best of them.

Despite all that time of prayer, I haven't really prayed as I should. I don't say this out of guilt or some misguided attempt to be holy. I say this because I am convinced, on almost a daily basis, that everything about my life would be better, different, and more God-directed if I spent more time praying and less time doing all the other things that occupy my time. I am convinced that more than anything else, I am called to prayer.

One of my favorite verses goes like this: "The first thing I want you to do is pray. Pray every way you know how, for everyone you know" (1 Timothy 2:1). It couldn't be simpler or more profound. I have copied this verse on note cards that I carry in my purse and car and have posted over my desk. I've memorized these words and repeat them to myself often. Still, I regularly forget to pray. I may be a reasonably intelligent person in some ways, but when it comes to prayer, I am seriously retarded. I know, without a shadow of a doubt, that the second half of my life must be guided, inspired, challenged, motivated, and powered by prayer. So why do I struggle?

I suppose it is similar to the challenge I face with maintaining my weight. When I think of all the diet books I have bought and all the low-fat, low-carb, and low-sugar foods I have tried, I wonder what my life would be like if

I had invested all that time and energy in prayer instead of dieting. It is embarrassing to admit that I have probably spent far more time in my life obsessing about my weight than practicing the presence of God in prayer.

Diets and prayer are similar in some ways. Both are deceptively simple, yet few of us stick with either one for long. Doctors agree that all diets follow a basic formula of cutting calories, and any theologian will tell you that prayer is simply talking to God. Like dieting, I find the study of prayer offers me examples of what others have done, and the small tips I discover through my study sometimes create an "Aha!" for me. So I have decided to make a habit of studying prayer as well as practicing prayer.

I have read books by great men and women of prayer like E. M. Bounds, Andrew Murray, and A. W. Tozer, as well as *Christian Prayer for Dummies*.[2] Through my reading, I have learned that different people pray in different ways, depending on their lifestyle, circumstances, personality, and the way their brains are wired. I have learned that some people can use the acronym ACTS (Adoration, Confession, Thanksgiving, Supplication) to frame their prayer life very successfully, while others, like me, find the formula stilted and frustrating.

I have learned to look for what works for me, as long as I keep talking to God. Just as some people swear by the Atkins diet, while others go to Weight Watchers, different types of prayer can be meaningful or frustrating. When I realize that I will be a student of prayer for the rest of my life, I am able to relax and feel less worried that I simply "don't get it." I give myself freedom to try different ways of praying without expecting that I should, by now, have attained some level of expertise that makes praying totally effortless.

My life is full of things that distract me from God, just as my weight is always at risk as I pass by the Häagen-Dazs ice cream on the way to buy frozen vegetables. I've learned certain patterns that work for me—like going to the store where the vegetables and ice cream don't share the same aisle—because I am not the most disciplined person in the world. So in this chapter, I will share some of the things I have learned about prayer, not as the formula that everyone should use, but as examples of how I have learned to pray.

SOME PERSONAL EXAMPLES

The first type of prayer I have learned that I need is what I call the "bookend prayer." I want to live every day within what I consider holy bookends. When the alarm rings in the morning, I turn it off and sink back down into my pillow for just a moment. As consciously as I can before drinking a cup of coffee, I pray, "This is your day, Lord. Take it and use me however you choose to do your will."

That's it. Nothing fancy or literary. Nothing so elaborate that I might be tempted to "get around to it later." My prayer is just a commitment that before my feet hit the floor, I have already handed the day back to God.

I am often reminded of this simple commitment when I have to make a decision during the day: "Lord, it's your day. What would you have me do?" It comes back to me when I am tempted to spend my time on something that is frivolous: "Lord, this is your day. How would you have me spend my time?" And I reaffirm it when I am stuck in traffic or frustrated by an outcome: "OK, Lord. I reaffirm that this is your day. I accept that this may be my day to learn humility."

At the end of the day, I spend another moment in prayer. Since I am one of those people who falls asleep almost before my head hits the pillow, keeping this prayer short is a necessity. "Thank you for this day, Lord. Please show me if I missed you somewhere in it." I admit that there are times when this prayer is not conducive to my sleep pattern. (If you suffer from insomnia, this might not be a good practice for you.) Even when I don't scroll through the events of the day or consciously make an attempt to remember, God will often bring someone to mind or replay a scene. Or sometimes I will have a dream in which I am reminded of an event or someone in need. It's not as if I am really seeking this type of insight. Usually, I am ready to drift off into unconsciousness.

Yet, time and time again, God has used this bookend prayer to let me know that there is some unfinished business in the day. A person will come to mind. Or a phrase from a conversation will be replayed. Or I will suddenly see myself rushing by someone who needed a little more attention. This is not a time when I get into petitioning God on behalf of someone else, nor do I typically act on the insight I receive. It's just a time to let God show me how the day went from his perspective. I'm often reminded that God's view and my view of a successful day are often quite different.

These bookend prayers are so simple that I really have no excuse to skip them. They are my baseline of prayer for the day. No matter where I am, no matter how busy or tired I may be, there's simply no way I can skip them. I have no idea why I didn't do this during my first fifty years. I tried at times, but sometimes it seemed too simple and other times too legalistic. But now I know that it's a matter of health and survival. I don't want to be wrestling God for each day. I'm no longer under the impression that I might have it figured out better than God. I don't even think that I might have more fun without God in the picture. (Now that's a sign of maturity.) I am ready and willing to surrender every day to God and to let him direct my path.

NOT-SO-QUIET TIME

I am not the quiet type. I don't like to sit still. If I am stuck
in a meeting or a lecture for too long, I get anxious and irritable. I was fifty before I realized I had all the symptoms
of ADD and had spent much of my life trying to avoid situations where I had to sit still and be quiet.

When I was growing up, my family attended a church
where the sermons often stretched for more than an hour.
I would fidget, daydream, draw, tap my feet . . . and invari-
ably be told to "sit still like a good girl." The fact is, I eventually began to hate church and even believed I wasn't holy
enough to be a good Christian. Then there was guilt I felt
for not wanting to have a "quiet time." To me, the active
fidgeter, the very phrase sounded like punishment or time-
out. I began to think of time with God as the equivalent of
time on a chair in the corner, a punishment that my father
discovered drove me to repentance faster than spanking.
So it is no surprise, I suppose, that I have struggled much
of my adult life to have what most Christians call a "quiet
time."

After years of trying to use the ACTS approach and finding myself drifting off during my attempts at prayer, I wondered if I was simply lacking something spiritually. But as I
learned more about myself, it became clear to me that the
very left-brained approach of the ACTS prayer was not
particularly engaging to my more visual brain. I learned

that I needed to approach God in a way that was meaningful to me, not in a way that fit someone else's formula.

I still try to make time for God first thing in the morning.
My time with God is best when I get up before everyone
else, but it doesn't always work that way. I've learned to
not be too hard on myself. If I have my time with God during lunch, I don't waste energy regretting my morning. I
know that I already handed the day over to God in those
very first moments of the day, and I'm now just improv-
ing upon it. I like to read a devotional or two, and I read
at least one chapter of the Bible. I try to pause and let
God speak to me through these sources, sometimes copy-
ing down a meaningful verse or writing in my journal when
something really strikes me.

I have created a prayer notebook that keeps me organized
and also serves as a source of inspiration. On days when I'm
discouraged, I can look back to "answered prayer" pages
and often be reminded of burdens I carried a year before
that have now been lifted. When I tell someone I will pray
for him or her, I try to write that down in my prayer journal
so I don't forget. I can't pray without a list, so my notebook
list is also transferred to a note card I carry with me, where
I only use initials in case it falls out of my purse.

Then I pray in a way I never did in the first half of my
life: I picture myself entering a lovely meadow, carrying a
basket and wearing a backpack. I come there and meet

Jesus. In my basket are flowers that I give to Jesus with words of thanks and praise. There have been days when I only had one flower in my basket, which I gave to Jesus to thank him for meeting me just as he promised he would. Other days, my basket contains a full bouquet of gratitude. I picture Jesus smiling as I hand him the flowers. Then I pull off my backpack and take out the rocks. I give him my burdens that are weighing me down. I give him the tiny, sharp stones that are irritating me. I give him the rocks that seem so hard they will never be cracked. I visualize handing these all over to Jesus, who takes them from me and then helps me put on my empty backpack.

I share this very personal imagery because it has changed my prayer life from a dreaded "quiet time" to a very fulfilling interaction with the Lord. It is simply a way in which I use my very visual sense to connect in prayer. This imagery may not work for anyone else, but it makes me anticipate my "walk in the meadow" and my "meeting with the Lord" as an active time rather than a passive event.

Some days, I do something that might seem odd to some people. I put my prayer list on the bookstand of my treadmill, and I jog while I go to the meadow. I find that the rhythm of my jogging helps me keep focused on prayer for a longer time. Often, I have to hold on to the sides of the treadmill because I get so caught up in praying that I lose my pace. Sometimes I look at the time and am surprised by how long I have been running or walking. Other days, I put on a Christian album and sing to God while I work out. I have a terrible voice, so this is best done when I'm alone in the house. If others are nearby, I listen to Christian music and at least hum along in praise.

The point is not to copy my example but to search for your own style and approach to prayer. God wants you to talk to him. He wants to talk to you. Work at finding the ways that are meaningful to you, and stop being stuck in ruts that don't work.

PRAYING FRIENDS

Another thing I have learned about prayer is the importance of praying with other people. Linda, Peggy, and I have been prayer partners for more than a decade. We've never lived in the same city, and Linda has not always lived in the same country. Sometimes we don't see each other for a year at a time. But we are always close because of our regular conference-call prayers. For years, we were on a very regular, every-other-week schedule. Now we tend to be less regular, although sometimes we pray more often when one of us needs support. Whoever has the conferencing facility at the time (and it seems like it has moved among us depending on job or telephone carrier) initiates the call and then brings the other person on the line. Each of us takes a turn talking about what is happening in our life, and then the others pray for the one who has shared.

What has been most amazing about this prayer friendship is how we are able to help each other see ourselves as God does. When one of us is discouraged about a long-term habit, the others can remind her of how far she has come with God's help. When one of us celebrates a victory, we all know how hard fought it was. When one of us is down, the others can list all the reasons that she is being way too hard on herself. When one of us is fretting over a child, the others will carry that child in prayer, often seeing him or her in a way a parent cannot.

Through the years, I've learned to turn to Linda and Peggy for advice, not only because I respect them but because I know they know me very well. They know my weaknesses and how God works in my life. And when they say they will pray about a struggle I'm having, I know they will. They will check up on me and hold me accountable in a firm but loving way. I love Linda and Peggy in a way that transcends time and circumstances, and I feel that they have been God-given friends. I can imagine us twenty years from now, still praying on the telephone together, although maybe by then we'll at least be able to see each other as we talk. We'll be praying for our grandchildren and probably still asking God to help us break some bad habit.

BE CAREFUL
WHAT YOU PRAY FOR

I have also learned that God sometimes uses my prayers to enable me to do things and go places beyond anything I could have imagined or planned. During the first half of my life, I was very big on setting goals. I had five-year goals, annual goals, monthly goals, and weekly goals. I had a daily to-do list that I updated carefully. I plotted my career, planned our vacations well in advance, and began to study college options as soon as my oldest son entered high school. When I look back on those goals, I realize that I generally made my plans and then asked God to bless them. My idea of how God worked meant asking him to help me achieve career plans and offering him a slot on my daily lineup. I was so driven and busy that whenever there was an unexpected change in my day, it really upended me.

One of the most surprising aspects of this new season of my life is a strange disinterest in goal setting. I'm just not sure where all those instincts went. The good news is that my goal setting has often been replaced by praying and a profound sense that if God doesn't set my goal, it isn't worth achieving. But I've also found that if God is in something, he takes it in a direction I might have never dreamed of myself.

The other day, someone introduced me as an AIDS activist. It wasn't a label I had thought to give myself, yet I
realized that much of my time during the past year had
been dedicated to HIV/AIDS issues. Just one year earlier, I
had been one of the many Americans who knew about
the pandemic but didn't know what it had to do with me.
I was aware that HIV/AIDS was a terrible global problem.
I had even visited African countries and seen the devastation brought on by the unimaginable number of deaths.
But like many people, I had felt overwhelmed and inca-
pable of making a difference. After all, I wasn't a doctor or
researcher. I couldn't invent a vaccine or treat the sick.

Then I was introduced to Robinah Bobirye, director of
the HIV/AIDS initiative for Opportunity International,
who was visiting Washington from Uganda. As we chatted
over coffee, I learned more about how the pandemic had
spread through her homeland of Uganda and how her fellow citizens had made remarkable strides in combating the
spread of the virus and reducing the infection rate faster
than any other nation in the world. Our conversation was
very informative—and then it turned personal. She told
me of the pain of losing her brothers and then her sister-
in-law, who was also her best friend. Almost in passing,
she mentioned that she was now raising nine children, one
of her own and the rest nieces and nephews orphaned by
AIDS. Her story touched me so deeply that I realized I had

tears in my eyes. And then I said something lame like, "I wish there was something I could do."

Robinah, in her soft but forceful way, said, "Of course there is something you can do. Pray. Ask God. He will show you." Robinah's story had touched me, so I did ask God to show me if there was anything I could do. I was thinking perhaps I could write a column for Religion News Service or maybe make a bigger contribution to an AIDS charity. Becoming an AIDS activist was not even in my wildest imagination. I was thinking on a completely different scale than God was. But I prayed, and I meant it. And God certainly answered.

I decided I should learn more about AIDS, so I started looking for a simple book. What I found were books that were large, complex medical tomes or books on some aspect of the politics of AIDS. I wanted the simple, basic facts. Surprisingly, nothing existed. I began to ask friends what they knew about AIDS; most knew as little as I did and confessed to having many questions and concerns. They, too, seemed to wish there was something basic to read. Many seemed skeptical that the AIDS crisis was as big a problem as it was portrayed to be. Others wondered why a "gay disease" was killing so many in Africa. Some offered bits and pieces of facts or fiction they had heard. The more I talked to people, the more determined I was to find out the facts. I was sure there was some simple source

of information. Yet the harder I looked, the more convinced I was that nothing existed.

Meanwhile, I had been praying that God would clarify
my career path. I was being offered jobs, but every one
seemed to come with a God-given warning. Why was God
closing so many doors that at first appeared to have my
name on them? I noticed in my journal that I was hearing an increasing number of signs that I was to do more
writing. But I didn't want to do more writing. I began to
whine to God that I wasn't a good enough writer. My writing was simple and basic, not beautiful and flowing. I might
be able to write simple newspaper columns, but I didn't
want to embarrass myself by actually proclaiming myself to
be a writer. Besides, writers had to sit still, and God knew I
wasn't good at that.

Then one night I was attending a Bible study when a
verse jumped out at me as if it was written in neon type.
We were studying 1 Corinthians 14 and the instructions
about prayer language. Then I came to verse 3: "But when
you proclaim his truth in everyday speech, you're letting
others in on the truth so that they can grow and be strong
and experience his presence with you." Suddenly I felt as if
God was taking all my whining and turning it back on me.
I wrote in everyday language, and that was just what was
needed to explain the AIDS crisis to others, especially to
those in the church. The very "handicap" that I felt was

keeping me from being a great writer was exactly what the church needed.

The circumstances that followed could only have been God directed. Normally it takes months to get a book proposal together, present it to a publisher, and wait for consideration. In June 2004, I made a telephone call and then put together a book proposal to write a very basic book addressing the questions the average person had about AIDS. It would be very simply written and designed in a very open, accessible format. I figured no publisher would agree to print such a book. It would never be a big seller, and it wasn't on a topic most people wanted to read about.

In a matter of days, I heard that the proposal would be presented to a publisher. There was just one problem: the publisher needed to know more about the format. Could I get some sample pages designed—in a few days? I called Ed Spivey, the talented designer at *Sojourners* magazine. Did he know anyone who could do such an impossible job? Ed agreed to do it himself. What he produced overnight was a stunning and accessible layout—exactly what I had dreamed it could be. I jumped on an airplane and flew to Atlanta to meet with the team at Authentic Publishing, the layouts of the pages in hand.

We came to a quick agreement on the book. But it would have to be written and produced in record time in order to distribute it for World AIDS Day, which was December 1.

Most books take about one year to produce. We were proposing to cut the entire schedule down to three months. It
meant I had only one month to write most of the content
and get it to Ed to start designing. *Impossible.* And even if
I could do my part, everything else would have to go exactly right.

Amazingly, it did. Three months later, *The Skeptics Guide
to the Global AIDS Crisis* was published.[3] We had little time
to advertise the book and barely any time to get it posted
on Amazon.com and other Web sites. But it didn't matter. It was the right time for a very basic book on AIDS.
Churches were waking up to the problem but needed a
basic book to distribute. Organizations raising funds for
AIDS needed to educate their donors. The book sold out
of its first printing in six weeks.

Doing research for the book made me more aware of the
issues regarding the global AIDS crisis. I wrote an article
for a magazine and then a column for AIDS Day. I began
to speak to groups that were interested in getting active.
I helped design a curriculum for schools. And I launched
the AIDS Orphan Bracelet Project. All of this happened
in the six months following my lame comment to Robinah
and her admonition to pray and ask God what he wanted
me to do.

I don't know if I have had a more productive six months
in my life. Yet the entire time, throughout all the craziness,

I rarely felt stressed or concerned that we might not make an impossible deadline or that the book would be a failure. I felt totally and completely that it was all God's doing. At some point, it occurred to me that if I had set out with the audacious goal to become an AIDS activist, I never would have dared to take on so many things or dreamed they would happen. I might have carefully listed my goals and objectives, developed timelines, and composed to-do lists. Even then, I don't think I could have come close to doing as much as God had in mind to do through me. I was simply along for the ride.

I've heard people describe me as "passionate" about fighting AIDS. It's true that I care deeply about educating Americans and helping meet the needs of those who are dealing with HIV/AIDS personally. But my passion is not the type of frenetic, aggressive sense I had when I was younger. This is a deep passion that comes from knowing I am part of a greater purpose. I do not have to make things happen. If someone asks me to speak about AIDS, I do. But I don't seek out opportunities or platforms. It's hard to feel we are making headway against this horrible disease, but that doesn't make me less passionate about fighting for progress. True passion, I have learned, prevails even when the circumstances are not exciting and the cause is not popular or glitzy.

I look back on that experience as a God-given glimpse of what he has in store for me. I know enough about publishing to know for sure that what happened was not humanly possible. Similarly, Naomi knew enough about her plight to know that she was not going to find her way without God. Yet when we come to him without our own plans and simply hand ourselves over, God is ready to show us what a great adventure he has for us. Prayer is how we find both purpose and passion.

Prayer is not something we do because we should. Prayer is our passport to the greatest adventure of our lives. If we do nothing else in the second half of life, we must learn to pray. In fact, I am beginning to believe that prayer itself is our primary second calling. Everything else is just gravy.

9. you've got to have friends

If prayer is the bedrock of the second half of life, then friends are the rich soil that gives form, substance, and richness to our calling. Friends, in my experience, are different in this time of life. The friendships are truer, deeper, and more involved while being, ironically, less complicated. In my second half of life, I am more inclined to value a friend for who she is and not over think the implications of our relationship. Any jealousy that once tainted friendships of my youth has long gone away. I can now honestly admire another woman's ability to do something better than me without a twinge of longing.

Many of the friendships in the first half of my life were almost a matter of proximity or circumstance. After leaving college, I became friends with neighbors, co-workers, and mothers of my children's playmates. Some of these friendships endured beyond the circumstances; many did not.

Some of the relationships were forged out of common frus-
trations or shared goals that changed with the situation.

I realize now that my life in the fast lane left little time
for friendships. In fact, friendships sometimes felt like a
burden; something I had to fit in on my to-do list. I was
not a very good friend to people who needed me. Their
neediness felt like one more demand, and I barely fit it all
in as it was.

I remember a time when a woman I barely knew at work
asked to go to lunch with me and then blurted out that she
wished she had more friends. I remember nearly choking
on my sandwich as I tried to encourage her to get out, take
a class . . . anything but look at me as a potential friend. I
was working so hard at that point that just going out for
lunch was a burden. Even my longtime friends were feeling
neglected during that time. I would sometimes call them
during my long commute; otherwise, they were lucky to
hear from me for months. I finally told the woman that I
made a lousy friend, looked at my watch, and said I needed
to get back to work.

Now I see how confused I was about the priorities of life.
I wish someone had told me that if I was too busy for
friends, then I was too busy. Maybe someone did, and I
just didn't hear them. I am pleased to see that many of
the younger women I know seem to be living their lives
differently and refusing to take on careers that crowd out

relationships. Perhaps they have learned from the examples of my generation.

Even in such a short book of the Bible, we learn that Naomi had friends. It's hard to understand how they stayed in touch when Naomi went to a far-off land for a decade. How can we imagine friendships without e-mail or cell phones? But her friends had known Naomi so well that when she returned, they not only recognized her but also saw that she was different. And Naomi was brutally honest with them. Instead of "spinning" her experience in Moab, she told them the truth about her misfortune.

FRIENDS WHO CONSOLE US

I am so grateful for my friends who have consoled and comforted me through difficult times. I've had some bad days in my life, but the day I turned fifty was one of the worst. I did not feel the kind of emotional pain I have experienced with deaths. I did not feel the horror of embarrassment or the devastation of failure. I felt mostly empty, useless, and unloved. My friend Betsy, who doesn't look a day over forty but has passed the midcentury mark herself, gave me a big hug and some great advice: "It's terrible. You're at rock bottom. No one can tell you it's not bad, because it is. So feel sorry for yourself for a day or two, then suck it up. Trust me, it doesn't get any worse than this."

Betsy was right on all counts. Now that I have come to terms with the fact that I am in the second half of my life, I feel surprisingly free. It hasn't just been because I've "sucked it up." I've learned from Naomi and other women that the second half of life is a journey unlike the first. Much of what I counted on to get me through the first half of life will do little to help me in the second. What comes next has to be viewed as an adventure. It is frightening, unsettling, uncomfortable, and unfathomable—but that's what the best adventures are like!

Friends like Betsy give me both encouragement and tough love. She and I had never met before our first day in the Community Bible Study group. I was just about to compliment her on her purse when she leaned over and said, in a lovely Southern accent, "I love your purse." We both laughed, and our friendship was off and running.

The women in our CBS discussion group became extraordinarily close as we studied the Gospel of John together. We laughed and cried and studied the Bible and prayed for one another. When Betsy's son was facing a difficult divorce, we prayed for him as if he was our own. When Marita tried to decide if she should return to work, we prayed as if our own careers depended on it. And although a number of us in the group were around the same age, three of the women were considerably older and offered us a shining example of elegance, humor, and joy in the years to come. The group provided a gift of friendships that remained long after we went our separate ways. I'm not sure how I would have made it through the first few days of being fifty if it hadn't been for Betsy and the others in my Bible study group.

I'd never had the time to be involved in a Community Bible Study group before. I'd made halfhearted attempts, but my schedule was so full that I never truly invested in the groups. So when I decided to sign up for CBS, I was determined to keep it as a firm date on my schedule. After the first few times, it became the high point of my week. The women from that group remain close, even though we have now all rotated into new discussion groups. We still have reunion luncheons from time to time and have a bond that has lasted well beyond that year's study.

FRIENDS WHO STRETCH US

In addition to the dear friends I have made in our Bible study group, I have also learned to appreciate the help and encouragement of friends who challenge me in other areas of my life. For example, three friends recently helped me accomplish something I could never have done alone—finish a 5K race.

Running had been part of my life for thirty years. Jogging, really. Nothing too intense, and always just for recreation or to try to keep my weight under control. My oldest son was the real runner, competing from eighth grade on in track meets and cross-country competitions. By the time I reached my fiftieth year, I was walking more than running, usually a couple of miles on the treadmill. So when my one-time walking friend Laura told me that she had started running again, I asked her if I could tag along. Sure, she said, but I'd have to be up and at the appointed meeting place at 6:00 a.m., rain or shine. She, along with Deb and Gigi, had a regular running appointment, since they were in training for a 5K. She sounded so serious that I almost backed out then and there. They had been training for the race for several months already, and I hadn't run more than two miles at a time for years.

The first morning out, I could barely keep up with them for the first half of the run. My treadmill workout was no match for the real streets, and I was never going to make it. I sat down on the side of the road and told them to go on without me. Fortunately, their course brought them back to the same point, so they picked me up and encouraged me to keep going. The second morning wasn't much better. But I enjoyed their company and reasoned that as long as I didn't hold them up, I would just run as far as I could and then rest until they doubled back. At least it got me up and exercising regularly.

A few days later, we were running and chatting when Gigi said to me, "Look, you're running much farther already."

She was right. As I talked with them and enjoyed their friendship, I forgot about the cramps in my legs. After two weeks, I could almost keep up with them, running farther than I had on my own. A few days later, I couldn't run in the morning, so I went out later in the day and ran the same route. I couldn't make it as far as I had the day before. It suddenly occurred to me that I was running farther *because* of my friends. For thirty years I had usually jogged alone, enjoying the solitude. Now I realized that running with my friends made a difference in my ability to actually cover the distance.

I still wasn't convinced I could run the 5K. A week before the race, I was barely running three miles and my pace was achingly slow. To run the race, I would need to pick up my pace and increase my distance. My friends assured me it was a piece of cake. It was hot and humid on race day, and I was already sweating as I walked to the starting line. It was a community race, so some of our neighbors, having watched our training, hooted and hollered at the "running ladies." We mugged back and posed for pictures with our arms around each other, hoping this wasn't the final picture taken of us before succumbing to heart attacks.

The course had never felt so long. We ran together for a while and then split up, running two by two. When one of us started to falter, the others encouraged her on. If one fell behind, another slowed down to keep us together. We all finished with times that might not have been spectacular but were not embarrassing. And for me the victory was most sweet: in my fiftieth year, I had run my first 5K.

This achievement made me feel victorious in a way that went beyond the race or running and gave me courage to face the years to come with optimism. Mostly, I realized how much I needed friends to get me through. Without Laura, Gigi, and Deb, I would never have finished the race; in fact, I wouldn't have even attempted it in the first place. I would have told myself I was too out of shape and too old. But my friends encouraged and helped me, and that made all the difference.

SPIRITUAL GROWTH FRIENDS

Another friend I treasure is Pam, who has been my partner in spiritual growth. Pam and I met just last year through mutual friends. When we got together for lunch one day, we discovered that we had many things in common. We might have gone shopping together or gone to a movie the next time we met, but we had both reached a point in our lives where we wanted to seriously follow God. We decided that our friendship would center on knowing and following God.

For the first time in my life, I have a friendship based solely on a shared desire to listen for God's calling in our lives. I have other Christian friends, and we often talk about how God is working in our lives. But Pam and I truly make an effort to keep our friendship focused on knowing God better. We go to Christian conferences, try out Bible studies, and share Christian books with one another. It's not that we never talk about anything else, but we do make an effort to spend most of our time concentrating on the Lord.

One day, we realized that we wanted to spend time together but we also wanted to exercise. So we came up with the idea to jog around the neighborhood and pray out loud. Pam lives about a mile south of me, so we set a point in-between to meet and begin our "prayer run" together. We felt a little silly at first, but then we figured most people would think we were just gossiping; and if they overheard us praying, what was the harm in that? It struck us as funny that we wouldn't be embarrassed if people overheard us gossiping, but we might be embarrassed for people to hear us praying.

As we ran through the streets, we prayed for the neighborhood in general and whenever we saw someone leaving their house, we prayed that he or she would get to work safely. We noticed a pretty flower garden and thanked God for the gardener. We saw toys strewn in a yard and prayed for a probably harried young mother. We jogged around Pam's church and prayed for the activities of the week and that many people would come to know the Lord. And then

we each jogged home—Pam running a few blocks south
while I ran a few blocks north—having accomplished our
exercise and having bonded in a way that went beyond a
shopping trip or a shared cup of coffee.

Our next goal is to start a prayer study group—a regular time to pray and to study prayer. Since neither of us has
ever tried this before, we are going to pray about who else
should come and what format the time should take. We're
not sure how much time we should study prayer and how
much time to actually pray, but we're sure that God will
show us.

Pam and I are fellow travelers on this journey. We gently
hold each other accountable and pray for each other regularly. We are determined to spend this part of our lives
growing closer to the Lord. As much as I admire Pam for all
the things she has accomplished and the other talents she
has, our friendship is based on spiritual growth.

"BEING JESUS" TO OTHERS

My friendship with Linda has opened up a new dimension
on friendship to me—the concept of "being Jesus" to others.
When I found out Linda was pregnant again, I admit I was
shocked. She was forty-five and had four teenagers. Yet
when I first met baby Isaac, I quickly fell in love. He was
a darling little towhead who got so much attention from
his big brother and sisters that he began to talk at an early

age and was counting to twenty before he was two. There seemed to be a full-grown man in that little boy's body! He had wisdom way beyond his years and a sense of humor that kept us all laughing.

Linda and I were in the Community Bible Study group together, studying the Gospel of John and the life of Jesus. One day, someone suggested that we should be going through each day asking, "How can I be Jesus to someone?" We were each personally challenged to take that phrase and pray about it.

Linda and I went to lunch that day, and she told me how sad she was that her mother's deteriorating mental and physical health prevented her from really knowing Isaac or being involved in his life as a grandmother. "Some days I wish I could just pick up the phone and tell my mom about some cute thing he did, just like I did with my other kids," Linda said. As I prayed that night for Linda, I began to have an idea. A few years older than Linda, I was old enough to be Isaac's grandmother. I could help fill in for Linda's mom. Being Jesus to Linda meant trying to love Isaac as a grandmother might.

From then on, I tried to look at Isaac with the love and delight a grandmother might have. I bragged about him and praised him extravagantly. With Linda's permission, I bought him an occasional present. I told Linda what a great mother she was and how well she was raising Isaac. I told

Linda that she should call me anytime he did something special, just as she might her mother. She should brag about Isaac to me, because I would love to hear about it. I was not just her friend; I was Isaac's surrogate grandmother.

Later, I learned that such investment in each other's lives can also be painful. When Linda's family decided to move to Africa, I was devastated. Not only was I losing my friend Linda, but I was losing my surrogate grandchild, Isaac, who had truly become the apple of my eye. Fortunately, Linda e-mails me regularly to share Isaac's antics, and I have another excuse to visit Africa soon.

My experience with "being Jesus" to Linda changed our friendship and my life. Now I try to remember to ask that question with each of my friends. How can I "be Jesus" to them? The question pushes me to a deeper level of love and care for my friends.

IT TAKES ALL KINDS

It's easy to be friends with people with whom I have a lot in common. But I have also felt that God wants me to go beyond my own little world in my friendships. Perhaps that's why he brought Helen into my life. Helen lived on the streets. I had seen her begging regularly as I passed through the Metro entrance on my way to work. But there was something different about her. Clearly, she had some physical problems. Her face was twisted as if from a stroke, and she walked with a profound limp. But there was nothing wrong with Helen's mind.

I passed her one day as I was hurrying to work, and she said, "New shoes. They look really nice with your coat." I looked up, startled and pleased that someone had noticed my new shoes. I had to laugh when I saw the source of the compliment. "Now that's better," she told me. "I knew I could get you to smile."

That was the beginning of what could only be described as one of the most unusual friendships of my life. Helen liked to talk. She rarely asked me for money, but she always asked for conversation. She knew when I rode the Metro home from work and would sometimes wait for me. There was nothing she seemed to enjoy more than a Metro ride and conversation. She knew that I often read the *Wall Street Journal* on the commute home, so she'd say, "Can I have the stock pages? I have to track my investments." People on the train would look at her, in her dirty disheveled clothes, and me, acting as if I was taking her seriously, and you could just imagine what they were thinking. Sometimes she'd string the joke out. "Wow. IBM just shot up again. Sure wish I hadn't sold my shares last month."

One day, she told me she was working on a book called *Washington, D.C., on a Dollar a Day.* She told me she intended to include a chapter about where you could find the best discarded food and what shelters offered the most

fashionable clothes. Helen had a great sense of humor and
an amazing amount of love.

One morning, I was in a hurry and not in a great mood. I
was rushing to the Metro and saw Helen out of the corner
of my eye. I was pretty sure she hadn't seen me, so I rushed
to the train, too tired and grumpy to engage in conversation. "I love you, Dale. Have a great day," she yelled to me
as I jumped on the subway.

Although she had a healthy disposition, Helen had serious physical problems. I asked if I could help take her to a
clinic, and she agreed. She told me that she had wanted to
go to the facility, but she had never been able to because
the Metro didn't stop nearby and no taxi would pick her
up. So I had Helen wait behind me while I hailed a taxi,
then she and I went to the clinic. I asked the people at the
clinic if I could cover some of Helen's medical expenses,
but they said there was little they could do for her. Most of
her problems came from permanent damage from at least
one stroke as well as another condition. She needed long-
term care and rehabilitation, and she'd need medical insurance to cover the enormous costs.

Another day, I took Helen to a shelter for women where
she could get counseling and find a warm bed for the night.
But she, like many women, was afraid of public shelters. I
talked to the counselor, and she told me that Helen could
choose to enter the welfare system, but that would mean

finding a regular residence so she could receive her checks each month. Helen was free to make her choice, and she preferred the streets. The counselor told me that Helen usually stayed in a house with a number of other women she knew. They all begged for enough money to pay the rent. It sounded like it was in a terrible part of town, but Helen assured me that she was fine.

One day I read about a house that had burned down, killing a number of "squatters." From the description, I feared it was Helen's house. And I never saw her after that day. My friend Helen was gone. For weeks, I wondered if I should have tried harder to help her. But I knew as much as I had tried, Helen had made her choices. I couldn't force her to change her lifestyle.

A few months later, I was on the Metro when a man came up to me and asked if I'd seen Helen. I asked him how he knew about her, and he said that Helen had been his friend too. He was the manager of a restaurant, and he always arranged to leave her a warm meal at a certain time. "I saw you on the Metro with her one time, and she told me about you. You were a good friend to her. None of us could persuade her to leave the life on the streets. But she actually had an amazing number of friends."

Standing there looking at this well-dressed man, it struck me as ironic that a homeless woman with profound physical problems had managed to be so attractive to so many people. Helen had simply cared about other people and offered an amazing amount of love. Our brief friendship taught me that it doesn't take much to be a true friend.

FRIENDS FOR LIFE

There are two elderly women who often sit in the pew in front of us at church. They sometimes whisper loudly to each other, sharing insights with anyone nearby. They make a cute and comical pair. Whenever I see them, I wonder who among my friends will stand the test of time. When I'm in my eighties, who will I still be whispering to or sharing my dreams with?

I feel fortunate that my spiritual assets include many wonderful friends. I am determined to make friendship a higher priority in the days to come. I want to be a better friend to those in my life, and I want to widen my circle of friends to include younger and older women who can challenge me in new ways. I look forward, someday, to enjoying the friendships of daughters-in-law and perhaps sharing grandmothering ideas with some of my friends.

I think of Naomi and her friendship with Ruth, and I pray that I can be that type of mother-in-law—such a good friend that even without the bond of marriage there is a continuing bond of love and loyalty. And I think of Naomi at the end of the Book of Ruth, triumphantly holding baby Obed while her friends praise her.

I know that friends can still draw me away from what is best, so I pray for both my friends and my friendships. I want them to be positive relationships that bring me closer to God and help me more fully realize my second callings. I want to live the rest of my life with the knowledge that friendships are far more important than jobs or titles or anything I may have valued so much in the first half of my life that I barely squeezed out time for my friends.

10. living in the present

Examining the circles I had drawn on the page, I contemplated their significance. After completing dozens of true/false and multiple-choice questions, I was now facing the more subjective portion of the test. The instructions said to draw three circles representing the past, present, and future. The introduction to the test encouraged spontaneity, rather than prolonged contemplation. So I had answered spontaneously—and was now reviewing my own response.

In college, I had been asked to do the same exercise, and I remember what my circles looked like then. The past was small, the present slightly larger, and the future circle was bigger than the other two combined. It was how I had viewed my life then and probably for much of my twenties and thirties. The future was a vast, open-ended possibility. The past wasn't of much interest, and the present was something I was going through on my way to the future. I spent much of the first half of my life zipping through the present as if it was something to be endured while I rushed toward the future, sort of the way I read highway signs for towns in Virginia when I'm en route to North Carolina.

But this time, my circles looked different: they were almost the same size. The past and future held nearly equal weight, my memories anchoring the past with a new sense of richness and appreciation. The future was less open-ended now. Aging was not just a vague possibility but a reality that framed and even fenced in all the wild and crazy dreams I once had for the future. I probably wouldn't be running off to Paris to live a bohemian life. I wouldn't be the first woman president, and my chances of earning a prize at Wimbledon were seriously in doubt. So were my fantasies of being a size four, speaking several languages, and becoming a peace negotiator. The future was no longer vast, uncharted territory.

Nestled between my more modest circles was the present. It was smaller, but it was holding its own in this new schematic. I was beginning to understand and appreciate the present in a way that I hoped indicated maturity and wisdom. "The Christian life can only be lived in the present," I once heard someone say, a statement that struck me with what I could only identify as Spirit-influenced force. I wrote that phrase in my journal and began to look for more understanding about its meaning.

A few years back, my then-pastor Craig Barnes preached a sermon that was so profound I listened to the tape of it over and over. The sermon was about manna, the heavenly food provided to the Israelites in the desert. With apologies to Barnes, who is a gifted preacher and lyrical writer, the main point I took away from the sermon was this: God gives us enough to make it through each day—nothing more and nothing less. Manna couldn't be hoarded or saved. Only enough could be collected for that day so it did no good to worry about the next day and whether the manna would come. You simply had to trust God.

One of the most fascinating and amusing parts of the sermon was the definition of *manna*. According to Barnes, the Hebrew word *manna* means, "What is it?" So, as he said, when kids would ask their mom, "What is it?" when she served them their manna, she would simply reply, "Yes." More seriously, manna offers us an example of how we are supposed to face each day: by asking God, "What is it?" To me, this has become a powerful, anchoring question.

Barnes's sermon came during an especially difficult period in my professional life, a time when each day seemed more overwhelming than the last. I learned to start my day by asking God to show me the manna, and day after day, he was faithful to provide it. Sometimes it came at the end of a long day. Sometimes I didn't see it until I dropped into bed and prayed to review my day, and God brought to mind some small glimmer of hope. Often the manna God provided was something small that I would have missed if I hadn't been looking.

During this time, I learned a profound lesson about living fully in the present. If I do not invest in it fully, live mindfully, and look carefully for that day's manna, I will miss it. Living in the present requires more discipline than the to-do lists and five-year plans for the future and more awareness than making photo albums and replaying tapes of the past. Living fully in the present means banishing "what if's" and "if only's" from my vocabulary and letting God do what he will with each day.

In his book *Everything Belongs*, Richard Rohr makes the spiritual case for living fully and completely in the present, in what he calls "the sacrament of the present moment." He says, "We cannot attain the presence of God because we're already totally in the presence of God. What's absent is awareness. Little do we realize that God is maintaining us in existence with every breath we take. As we take another it means that God is choosing us now and now and now."[1] Like the search for manna, Rohr suggests surrounding every circumstance with the awareness that God has brought it into our lives for a reason. There is no random act or accidental circumstance. Everything is there to teach us, to provide an opportunity or to simply witness to God's presence. In short, everything belongs.

I explained this concept to my son Tyler, and he has embraced it with enthusiasm. When I get frustrated, Tyler will often say to me, with his gentle humor, "Remember, Mom, *everything belongs*. Even that guy who pulled out in front of you."

PRESENT TENSE

On my way to the airport one day, a rainstorm hit with a vengeance just as I pulled out of the driveway. I sat on the Beltway, barely inching along as the time of my departure grew closer and closer. "Please, God, delay the plane," I prayed, even as I recognized that I should have left sooner. I was especially anxious because I was flying to Dallas for a meeting but was taking a plane that would get me there in time to see my dear friend Peggy and carve out a few hours for us to catch up over dinner. I really, really wanted to make that plane. By the time I arrived at the airport, my plane was due to depart. I parked quickly, dashed to the counter, and asked if there was a chance I could still make it. "Nope. That's the only plane to actually depart on time," the woman told me as I looked at a screen filled with "delayed" notices. "The next flight leaves in two hours—if it's on time."

At times like that, I have learned to repeat the phrase as a calming prayer. *Everything belongs. Everything belongs. Show me, Lord, how everything belongs . . .* I managed to smile at the woman and thank her for the information. Then I asked if she would kindly book me on the next flight. She hesitated, and I remembered that in an effort to save money I had booked the flight through an on-line ticket service. It was my own fault that I'd missed the flight, and the airline had no obligation to put me on another one without charging me.

Maybe the fact that my hair was dripping on her counter made her want to move me on. Or maybe the fact that I had shown less frustration than I normally would have made the woman want to help me. In any case, she booked me on the next flight, and I was left to wander Baltimore-Washington International Airport in shoes that squeaked and hair that looked as if I'd just jumped out of the shower.

I called Peggy, apologized, and bought a cup of coffee. Silently, I prayed for God to show me his purpose in the delay. *Was I there to speak to some lonely soul?* I smiled at a woman who was trying to manage two small children, thanked the woman who gave me change, and tried to look pleasantly available. No one spoke to me. I decided that maybe I was supposed to speak to someone on the airplane. When I finally boarded, I had a sense of anticipation. The teenager who sat down next to me barely looked at me before falling asleep. By the time I finally arrived in Dallas, Peggy and I had just enough time to grab a quick meal before a restaurant closed.

Since Peggy and I have been prayer partners for many years, it's natural for me to share my failings with her. I told her how disappointed I was about missing the plane and missing the opportunity to spend time with her. And I also confessed that I was a little disappointed that God hadn't shown me a purpose in the delay. I hadn't been able to help anyone or be an encouragement. My delay hadn't been used for any good purpose.

"Dale, look at you," Peggy said. "You're calm. You don't sound like you were irritated or upset at the ticket counter. You smiled at people instead of rushing by them. You didn't stamp around the airport for two hours being cranky. It was raining and people were late and missing flights, and you might have been the nicest person the lady at the counter met. You might have been the only person to smile at the security screener in an hour."

Peggy hadn't read Rohr's book at that point, but she got his point better than I had. Living expectantly in the present is its own reward. Looking for God's purpose in a missed flight or traffic jam or cranky e-mail changes everything. It's not that we are being dropped into some heavenly drama already in progress. We don't find purpose by being used by God in some miraculous intervention or to be his stand-in because he needs our assistance to help someone. We are called to abide in him, to live in communion with him. We are called to practice the presence of God, whether it gets noticed or not. It is enough—and everything—to belong to God and know it.

A few weeks later, I was in an airport purchasing a snack to take on a flight. As the woman took my money, she asked, "Are you a Christian?" I couldn't have been more shocked. My mind was on the meeting I was flying to attend, and I doubted I was smiling or looking particularly angelic. In fact, when I'm deep in thought, I often frown. "How can you tell?" I asked, knowing I wasn't wearing my cross necklace or any religious symbol to tip her off. "I can just tell," she said with a smile.

Maybe she asks everyone that question, but I have to say it made me wonder why no one in an airport had ever asked me before. For years, I was one of those people who saw airports as places to get through on the way to somewhere. Now I realize that God can provide manna even in a bustling airport, and that has certainly changed my perspective. Maybe I'm a bit calmer now. Or maybe I'm just training myself to look for God's presence.

GOD IN PRIME TIME

One of my favorite television shows was *Joan of Arcadia*. Perhaps it's strange that a middle-aged woman enjoyed watching a show about a high school student, but the show was really about how God works in our everyday lives.

In the show, God appears to Joan in different forms, sometimes as a punked-out guy with spiked hair or a lady in the cafeteria or even a child on the playground. Once Joan starts to realize how often God shows up in human form, she begins to mistakenly think that anyone who appears in her life may be God. This leads to some confusion, but it also gives her a whimsical view of people that few of us have. God often asks Joan to do something unusual— go to work on the school yearbook, try out for a part in a play, or join the chess team. She's never sure why. She often tries to guess God's purpose in her assignment, but she almost always gets it wrong. God's purpose is always much bigger or much smaller than Joan realizes. Sometimes she's only had a bit part in a much bigger drama. Sometimes God just wanted her to sing a song or discover a poem in the trash can or be a friend to someone who was lonely.

Even though Joan is less than half my age, I identify with her notion of God and his purpose. I want to know what it is I am being called to do, and mostly I am beginning to understand that I will never know. As someone has wisely said, "The going is the way."

PACKING IN THE PRESENT

My involvement in the AIDS Orphan Bracelet Project has given me a new perspective on the importance of living in the present. One evening, I was packing envelopes well after my husband went to bed. "I'll be up in a while," I told him, as I put labels on the mailers. Our family room contained five thousand bracelets that had just arrived from Uganda. On the floor was a pile of e-mail orders from churches, schools, and individuals who had heard about the AIDS Orphan Bracelet Project and wanted to get involved. Next to me was a growing pile of boxes and mailing envelopes I would carry to the post office the next day. I was tired, and I'd just cut my finger on a mailer. *I didn't think it would be like this*, I prayed a bit petulantly.

Several months before, I had asked God to help me know what I could do to help fight the AIDS plague sweeping Africa. One day, I was in my Bible study when some women noticed the attractive beaded bracelet I was wearing from Kenya. They talked about the beautiful colors and the intricate beadwork, and they said they would all love to have a bracelet like that. The next week when I came to the Bible study, I told them about my AIDS book. They were polite, but AIDS was not something they really wanted to talk about first thing in the morning. I went home that day and asked God to show me how to communicate to these women and others about

AIDS. I knew they had good hearts, but somehow I wasn't getting through.

This was before the days of the Lance Armstrong brace-let, but I did remember the POW bracelets we wore during the Vietnam years. And I remembered how the women had admired my African bracelet and were willing to talk about it. Maybe there was some way to bring the two to-gether. Before I went any further, I prayed. I asked God to show me clearly if I was to move forward and pursue this idea. I knew that my marketing and entrepreneurial ten-dencies could get me way ahead of God if I wasn't careful.

I began to make a list of all the things I needed. I wouldn't want to spend money on promotion or mailings, so I'd need to set up a Web site. I'd need one that was easy to find, but I also knew that Web addresses had been grabbed by just about every organization around. So I asked God to show me if I should move forward by the availability of a Web address. I was amazed to find www.aidsbracelets.org was available as a domain name. I sent through my credit card number and reserved it.

Where would I get the bracelets? I talked to my friends at Opportunity International, and they put me in touch with their partner organization in Uganda. Eventually I found Gloria, a widow who supported four AIDS orphans and headed a microenterprise group of women who made bas-kets, placemats, and jewelry to support themselves, their families, and the AIDS orphans they had taken in. The Internet made it possible for me to send an idea for a sample bracelet through to the group. But the cost of the bracelets and the shipping was more than I had anticipated. I could put some of my own money toward the project, but I didn't want to ask people for donations and then deduct the cost of bracelets from them.

My friend Michelle Conn, who is an experienced fundraiser, offered to help me write a grant proposal. I talked to various churches and found that they really wanted to help connect their people with the AIDS crisis. But they didn't want to support just one organization, and they didn't want to feel like a group was fund-raising at the expense of support for the church. They wanted a simple project that could raise funds for support of AIDS orphans and would benefit more than one ministry. So before I could develop a proposal, I had to find out what ministries the project would benefit.

Opportunity International was doing some work in training AIDS orphans to have a marketable skill, and they were happy to be included. They were already working in partnership with Compassion International to take some of their older sponsored children into the program. Compassion was administering anti-retroviral drugs to AIDS orphans in Uganda, a program that was unique and in need of funds. Compassion also wanted to be involved. As a board member of International Justice Mission, I knew of their work in Uganda and Zambia to help protect the rights of widows and orphans who were HIV-infected.

I went to several other organizations that were working with AIDS, but they either couldn't commit to having funds go to AIDS orphan work or weren't interested. World Vision, with its huge humanitarian relief program, probably wouldn't want to cooperate with the rest of the smaller groups, I thought, but I asked anyway. I was thrilled when they were willing to join in and cooperate equally with much smaller ministries.

We had the ministries on board, and we knew where to get the bracelets. Now there was the matter of funding. Michelle helped write a great proposal and suggested some foundations that might be interested in supporting the cause. After all, they would give the seed money for a project that could take their investment and see it quadruple or more in benefiting four outstanding ministries. And the initial investment would support the group making the bracelets. Although some foundations liked the idea, each seemed to have a reason why they couldn't fund it. But a month later, the SAJE Foundation gave a grant to the AIDS Orphan Bracelet Project and we were up and running.

But each day brought new challenges. I needed a non-profit entity to accept the grant, but creating one would involve more cost and accounting fees and other expenses

I wanted to avoid. I didn't want to set up an organization or create an infrastructure. I wanted the whole thing to be as simple and transparent as possible. After many false starts, I was lead to the National Christian Foundation, and they agreed to administer the account. That was my manna one day.

Then I went to the bank one day to wire funds overseas and was told that under the Homeland Security Act, I couldn't wire money overseas without a great deal of paperwork to prove I wasn't funding a terrorist group. Each time something like that happened, I went back to God and asked him if he was shutting this door. Was I only called to take this project so far? Was I being taught humility? Every time I encountered an obstacle, I tried to wait and pray instead of resorting to my old habits. And each time, God provided a wonderful and unexpected solution. I had never felt so much like I was called to just live in the present and not worry about the next step.

Then the exciting day arrived. The post office called to say they had several large boxes for me from Uganda. But they were suspicious. The post office needed me to come in person and allow the boxes to be inspected. Tyler had just come home from school and agreed to go with me to the post office to help bring the bracelets home. When they took us to the back room at the post office, we could see

the problem. The bracelets had been packaged in old boxes, some of them marked with Arabic writing. In Washington, D.C., post-9/11 and the anthrax scare, they couldn't
be too careful. Fortunately one box had burst open, and
they could see the harmless bracelets inside. But when
I saw the contents, my heart sank. The bracelets I had ordered were distinct. They were black wooden beads with
red, yellow, and green beads at intervals. These bracelets
all appeared to be different. The ones I saw were pink and
green.

As Tyler helped me load the boxes into the car, I told
him that I was afraid they had sent the wrong bracelets. I
refused to look inside all the boxes for fear I would discover I had thousands of bracelets in the wrong colors. What
would I do? The Ugandan women had spent the time and
needed the income. I thought I had been very clear about
what I had ordered. I couldn't send them back or refuse to
pay. "Let's pray, Tyler," I said as I drove out of the post office.
"Let's ask God to heal the bracelets," I said, half joking.

Tyler laughed and reminded me, "Remember, Mom, everything belongs." He was right, of course, but the bracelets
were all wrong. Our first order gave us seven thousand
bracelets in a wide assortment of colors. Few were alike.
Hardly any had the distinctive red, yellow, and green that
symbolized AIDS, hope, and abundance. "Out of our

abundance we give hope to those with AIDS," I had posted on the Web site. I tried to imagine how we would make sense of this cacophony of colors and designs.

Eventually, it became clear that I would have to order again and be very clear about what I meant. I planned a trip to Uganda to meet with the group and be sure they understood what we wanted. In the meantime, seven thousand bracelets took up a corner of the family room. Tyler smiled every time he looked at them. I wanted to cry.

Then the orders began coming in. I had to buy packing materials and learn the best way to send various quantities. I had to figure out an economical way to send materials. And I realized that I had no idea how I would keep up with the demand. I had visions of Lucille Ball in the *I Love Lucy* episode when she is trying to keep up with the items coming at her on a conveyor belt. Every time I felt anxious, I got on my knees. "This is your project, Lord," I would pray. "If I am supposed to fail miserably and learn humility, I accept that. Just help this make a difference in people's hearts, and let it truly help AIDS orphans."

My trip to Uganda was life changing. When I saw how many orphans there were in the country, I knew I had to do something to help. Almost everyone I met had taken additional children into their homes, straining their already meager budget. Gloria greeted me with a huge hug and showed me the new bracelets she and her group were stringing. They were perfect, exactly the design I had ordered, and ready to be carried home in the extra suitcases I had brought along. She apologized for the confusion about the other bracelets but was greatly relieved that I was still willing to pay for them. As I sat in her simple home and saw how hard she worked to care for her own children and four AIDS orphans, it seemed ludicrous that I would consider the purchase of that first group of bracelets to be a mistake. Surely God would help me figure out what to do with them.

While I was gone, an article appeared in *Sojourners* magazine about the bracelets, and I received dozens of orders in a few weeks. I spent hours packing bracelets and sending them to schools and churches. As AIDS Day approached, the word had spread and everyone wanted quantities—within a few days. Then people wanted them for Christmas fairs at churches and Christmas presents for their friends.

I could barely keep up. But I always did. It was as if God knew exactly how many I could package up and send out each day. Some people asked me why I didn't do a promotional campaign, since my professional background included public relations and advertising. The fact is, I have felt strongly that God wants this to be a grassroots effort, not something that becomes a popular cause but a tool he can use.

I don't want to become known as the person who started this project. None of it could have happened without help from so many people along the way. Some people ask me why I don't hire someone to package the bracelets. The reason I don't is that for now I feel called to sit on the floor of my family room and practice the presence of God as I pack the bracelets. It is a humbling and very rewarding task. As I pick up each bracelet, I know it was made by a woman or girl who has had a much more difficult life than I have; and as I send out each package, I know that whoever wears the bracelet may be changed by this simple expression of support.

Mostly, though, I have never done anything in my life that has been so beyond my control and taught me more clearly that I am to rely on God every day. So far, thousands of dollars have been raised for AIDS orphans. I'm thrilled about that. But whether the money comes in or doesn't is in God's hands. The bracelets go out to anyone who asks for them. No bill is sent out, just an envelope for returning the donation. If someone takes bracelets and doesn't return any donation, no one follows up. It is totally an honor system.

Some days, I whine to God about being tired of doing the grunt work. Some days, I cry as I open the mail and find a generous donation or a heartfelt letter from someone who has been touched and wants to help. But every day, I hand the project and myself over to God and ask him to give me enough manna to get me through the day. Nothing more, or I'll get ambitious. Nothing less, or I'll feel afraid. And so far, each day he has given me just enough to live in the present.

11. passing it on

Naomi and Ruth's relationship is a compelling example of successful mentoring. The friendship between the older woman and her younger daughter-in-law is one of companionship and nurturing. Of course, their story is much more than that. Ruth's devotion to Naomi was not just about her love for Naomi but also her love for Naomi's God. The drama played out was much bigger than the relationship between the two women, and Naomi's advice to Ruth would have meant little without divine involvement.

Clearly, we can learn from the way Naomi taught Ruth and the ways in which she encouraged and prepared her for the journey to Bethlehem. Naomi knew all about being a foreign woman in a land where the customs were strange and rarely favored women. She had spent her early married years negotiating the unfamiliar customs of Moab and

raising her sons in a culture that was different than what
she knew. She'd probably made her share of blunders and
even found herself being jeered by men who didn't appreciate this foreign woman in their land. She not only wanted
to help Ruth feel comfortable in Bethlehem, but she certainly wanted to save her some of the pain she must have
experienced herself. Naomi understood that the best mentoring comes out of places of pain and hurt in our own life.

FOREIGN WOMAN

The first time I went to a Muslim country, I realized just
how very foreign a woman can feel. I had read a book
about the customs of Mauritania and knew the basic Arab
greeting: "Salaam Aleikum." I knew my left hand should
never be used for eating or greeting anyone, and I should
try to keep my head covered. I packed only long skirts and
shirts that would cover most of my arms, despite the intense heat. I felt prepared.

But nothing about Mauritania related to my experience.
I knew this from the moment I looked out of the airplane
as the pilot announced our final approach. We'd been flying over nothing but desert for miles, and in the distance
it appeared that the ocean simply met the desert with no
break between the white sand and the blue waters. *Where
is the city?* I wondered. Even as the plane bumped down on
the runway, I saw little besides sand on either side. I later

heard that the runway itself is often covered by sand and has to be swept off so approaching airplanes could land.

Life in the desert was totally different than I had imagined. As we set out from Nouakchott, our driver, Malik, stayed on the paved road for a short time until it was lost to the drifting sand. Then he veered off and followed a faint and intermittent track in the sand. I panicked. In my halting French, I asked him where we were going. He laughed. "Kiffa!" he said with delight. I knew that Kiffa was our intended destination, but I could only pray that he knew how to get there as we rolled over sand dunes, passing an occasional herd of camels. Obviously, Malik wasn't following a road map, and the sand looked all the same in every direction. The sun was exactly overhead, and I saw no compass. Fortunately I was with some World Vision staff members, and they assured me that Malik was one of the best local drivers and that I could trust him with my life. I realized that I would have to, whether I liked it or not.

Nine hours later, we pulled in to Kiffa as a magnificent sunset illuminated the tents that were the primary shelters of the nomadic population. Clearly, we weren't going to find a Holiday Inn in this place. I was so far out of my comfort zone I didn't even know what to worry about. But Malik had the arrangements all worked out. I had a comfortable bed for the night, and once the sun went down, the temperature dropped below 100 degrees.

Over the next days, Malik took me wherever I wanted to go, generously introducing me to his family and a women's group making crafts. The women taught me how to drape gauzy fabric over my head and around my waist to create a malafa, the traditional dress of Mauritanian women. The malafa kept out the swirling sand and protected me from the intense sun. It also helped me look the part of a modest Muslim woman.

One woman did an elaborate henna design on my hands, painstakingly creating the beautiful scrollwork with a razor blade and paper before packing my hands with henna and then wrapping them in plastic to "cure." When they unwrapped my hands and washed them off, I was tattooed with an exotic design similar to what many of the women wore. I learned to drink the traditional three cups of tea, each a bit stronger than the last, without grimacing or choking on the final brew. I sat on my left hand during meals, just to be sure I never used it by mistake. I began to feel more confident about fitting in.

Then one day, I asked Malik if I could go to the market. I should have realized that his polite desire to please me was being tempered by concern. "Oui," he replied, hesitantly. "You must stay very close to me," he added, frowning as if to indicate my idea was not such a good one. When we entered the market, I quickly realized that it was almost all men. I was a foreign woman among dozens of males who

stopped talking as I passed by, not with interest but disap-
proval. I was invading their territory. I pulled the malafa
closer to my head and wrapped it across my face, remembering to cast my eyes downward as I searched the market
for interesting items.

Then everything happened at once. A friend spotted
Malik and called to him. He turned just as a strong wind
blew through the streets, grabbing my malafa and making it into a kite that swirled behind me. I was still totally
covered underneath by my skirt and blouse, but my light
hair and face were suddenly exposed, and my inexperience
with my malafa allowed it to completely unwrap in sec-
onds. Suddenly the men around me who had silently put
up with my intrusion jumped up and began to jeer at me.
One spit in my direction. I grabbed at the fabric, tried to
rub the sand out of my eyes, and frantically searched for
Malik. I was terrified, knowing that I was breaking several
customs at once and being sure that the men in the market cared little that I was an American citizen or a member
of the World Vision board or knew a good lawyer. I was a
foreigner, making a mockery of their customs and view of
modesty. It passed through my mind the penalty for my in-
discretion might be stoning.

Malik grabbed up the yards of cloth that had once been
wrapped around me and, with a firm hand on my elbow,
ushered me out of the market and back to the car. He

looked very serious until we had the market in our rearview mirror and were half a mile away. I had not only endangered myself but caused him concern.

He said nothing until we reached the group of women who had sold me the fabric. Then he opened the door of the car and said something to the women. Their eyes opened wide when they heard him tell the story, and they laughed. They began to painstakingly teach me, once again, how to wrap my mulafa so it held securely even in the winds of the desert. It took several more sessions before I could walk around without gripping the fabric so tightly that I couldn't do anything else.

No matter how confident I felt in my own country, I was so clueless I was dangerous in Mauritania. Even though most of the people were wonderfully welcoming, I had to depend on the kindness of strangers and my guide, Malik, to keep me out of trouble. Perhaps the feelings I had were similar to those experienced by Naomi when she first came to Moab—and by Ruth when she entered Bethlehem.

We know that Ruth had to quickly figure out a way to find food for herself and her mother-in-law. She was at the mercy of those gleaning in the fields to allow her, a foreign woman, to join in and search for the meager rations. This practice must have been strange to Ruth, who presumably never had to beg for food in her bountiful homeland. Gleaning for food must have been not only humiliating but potentially hazardous, since when Boaz noticed Ruth, he asked his workers not only to allow her to reap but also to protect her. The famine in Judah was only recently over, and many hungry and poor people must have been competing for the leftovers from the harvest.

Ruth was not only poor, but she was a foreigner attached to an older woman who had come back to Bethlehem. She must have felt like I did that day in the Kiffa market. She had no context and no reason to believe others would look on her kindly. She didn't even know what customs she might be breaking or whether the owner of the land she had happened upon was friendly or hostile. She must have hoped for nothing more than to lay low, keep from being noticed, and work hard enough to collect a meager ration for her and Naomi.

A WORD FROM THE WISE

When Ruth returned to Naomi with her bushel of grain, Naomi immediately recognized that something big was going on. She may have told Ruth to go out and gather grain, but she hadn't told her where to go. So when Ruth told her about the man who had not only let her glean in his field but also showed her favor, Naomi didn't try to take any credit or set a plan for the future. She instead stopped to recognize God's hand in the process and acknowledge that he hadn't forgotten them after all. In doing so, Naomi passed the first test of a good mentor: she didn't try to foster dependence on herself. Naomi would only mentor her daughter-in-law within the context of God's will. She didn't know if that meant Ruth would flourish while she remained alone. She was willing to put Ruth's needs ahead of her own.

As I look back over the years, I realize how many older women gave me a word of advice, a note of encouragement, or a subtle arm around the shoulder. Every time I open my recipe box and see my favorite chicken recipes (all provided by my mother) or advise my sons on some bit of etiquette (also taught to me by my own parents), I recognize how much I still rely on the wisdom of those who came before me.

My generation had few women mentors at work, so many of my professional advisers were men. But I benefited from women like Colleen Evans and Roberta Hestenes, who served on the World Vision board with me and provided wonderful examples of grace and strength. I have discovered that mentoring is especially powerful when there is a spiritual component to the relationship.

MENTORING BY ACCIDENT

Sometimes a mentoring relationship is formed quite by accident, as it did in my relationship with Amy, a bright and energetic young woman I met at our church.

The newly formed committee at our church was called the Bosnia task force. The war in the Balkans was in the news, and members of our church wanted to do something to respond. So the missions committee had formed a task force to look at our options. Since I was the only member of the committee who had actually been to Bosnia, I was quickly drafted as a cochairperson. When Amy walked in to one of our first meetings, it was clear that she was going to be a stellar committee member. A beautiful young woman, she quickly got to the heart of every issue, asking questions that moved the committee forward and offering creative suggestions for our approach. *She's our next chairperson*, I thought with a sense of excitement and relief. By then, I had held enough leadership positions to know I would be happy to get the committee started and hand it off to someone else.

Amy did, in fact, become chair of the task force, propelling it forward to such creative heights that our church hosted a national forum on Bosnia with a star-studded panel and sent mission teams to work on various projects that have made a lasting impact on the country and our congregation. Meanwhile, Amy became my friend. We worked just a block away from one another and began to meet at the Starbucks across the street from her office to talk about Bosnia, work, and her dating life. I encouraged her through failed romances and dreadful dates. I offered some advice on her career (although she seemed to be heading for the top faster than I could comprehend), and together we searched for ways to bring our faith into our lives.

Amy joined our family for Thanksgiving dinner one year when she couldn't go home (the year we lost power and had to cook the turkey on the outdoor grill while I melted the arm of my ski jacket). She later told me that my example of laughing off the disastrous meal had given her courage to entertain even when things didn't go well at all.

Eventually, Amy married the man of her dreams, moved to Seattle, and started a family of her own. And when the International Justice Mission board was looking for a new woman board member who had both creative skills and a love of the developing world, it was easy for me to recommend Amy. Now we serve together on that board, and I get the pleasure of hearing about Connor's first words and seeing pictures of him as he grows up. I was able to comfort Amy when she lost a baby and to share the joy of her becoming pregnant again.

When Amy recently introduced me as her mentor, I was actually surprised. It always feels to me like I'm learning more from Amy than she will ever learn from me. Ours is simply a friendship between women who are fifteen years apart in age but share many of the same life experiences and passions. I certainly never set out to be Amy's mentor, and it's not anything I have sought in any formal way. But

Amy's friendship is special to me. I have watched her grow into a seasoned professional, wife, and mother, and part of me marvels at how she handles it all so much more gracefully than I did. She knows that I have experienced the everyday challenges of balancing a career and family and also knows that I understand the pain of losing a baby. Our friendship has been a blessing to both of us, as we learn from one another in different seasons of our lives.

A GROUP TO MENTOR

Effective mentoring relationships can also be formed in a group of women who share common interests or experiences and meet regularly to help and encourage one another. One day, my friend Karen, who used to work for me, shared with me about her struggle to stay motivated as she raised money for a ministry. Not long afterward, I was talking to another friend, Carrie, and it occurred to me that she and Karen might benefit from knowing one another. A few weeks later, I was in an advisory board meeting when Randi, a young woman development officer at that organization, sought me out for advice.

It was too much of a coincidence. All of the women were under thirty-five and were in development positions for major Christian organizations. So I called each and suggested a date in the near future when they and anyone else they knew in a similar position could come over to our

house for a chili dinner and conversation. I would provide
the place and the food and help frame the conversation.
They were just there to meet one another and see if they
could form a "young women's group" to help and encourage one another.

We ended up having a few dinners, usually attended by
half a dozen women. I would throw out a question about
how they dealt with their work or balanced work with their
personal lives, and the conversation would be off and running. I wasn't really there as a mentor but more as a cata-
lyst to bring these young women together and provide the
space to see what God might do. I loved watching them
help each other make connections, share war stories, and
provide resources to each other.

It occurred to me that the model of our chili dinners
could work for anyone who is willing to bring together a
group of women who share experiences or simply want to
learn a skill. Maybe a woman who knows how to knit could
offer to teach other women. World Vision's Women of
Vision groups usually start as a group of women who
want to know more about poor women in the developing
world and undertake a six-week study together. Many of
them grow into much more, but every woman who starts in
a group begins with the simple desire to learn more about
women in the developing world.

Of course, more traditional Bible study groups can also

be a wonderful way to bring women together and let older women pass on their knowledge to younger women. But I've found that most of us expect someone else to start a Bible study or want to join a large, organized group.

Years ago, I interviewed Anne Ortlund, the author and speaker who had written the classic book on spiritual mentoring, *Discipling One Another.*[1] I was amazed to learn that Anne had taken on the concept of spiritual mentoring so seriously that each year she took a group of women under her spiritual wing. After twenty years, the fruits of her labor were more than six hundred women! She hadn't taught each woman herself. She started out with three women; then the next year, she discipled five. Her principle was simple but firm: every woman she discipled then had to go on and teach another. The six hundred women who gathered one day to honor Anne were first-, second-, and third-generation disciples.

When I learned about Anne's incredible ministry, I told her I wished I lived in Southern California so I could join one of her groups. She looked at me with kindness but firmness and said, "You need to start a group yourself."

I backpedaled like crazy, thinking of all the reasons that I couldn't teach others. So Anne put it simply: "Do you know one Bible verse?" Of course I did. I think I managed to nod. "Then teach that verse to someone," she said. "Then the next week, you'll have to learn another so you can teach a new one." Anne's challenge made me ask God to show me whether there was some possibility that I could actually start a group. After all, my schedule was crazy, I didn't feel adequate . . . I had a million reasons.

A few weeks later, Becky Pippert, an author and wonderfully gifted Bible teacher, called to say that she was thinking she wanted to start a Bible study. Since moving to the Washington area, she had been thinking about getting one together and wondered if I'd like to help. I was happy to offer my house as the location, as long as I didn't have to teach. She was willing to teach the study, so we agreed to pray that God would bring the right people together. We ended up with five women, all professionals, who were available to meet one evening a week. None of them had spent much time in church or had any formal Bible training. But they were eager to study the Gospel of John together.

Everything went well until Becky called one week to tell me she was going out of town unexpectedly. "No problem. We'll just cancel," I suggested. But she was insistent that we not break the routine the other women had come to expect. The only way to move forward was if I led the study.

I was terrified. I knew I'd make a fool of myself. I worried that the women would be turned off to the Bible forever after listening to me. I don't know if I've ever studied the Bible as hard or prayed as much as I did that week. But when the time came, I felt calm. I had learned a tremendous amount and was thrilled when the women in the group joined in. By the end of the evening, one of the women asked if I would consider teaching the group more often.

I'm sure I wasn't close to being as gifted a teacher and speaker as Becky. But I did know that God had given me the grace and insight to get through that evening and to show me that we don't need to teach someone else under our own power. He is there, waiting and willing to provide the necessary resources.

SETTING THE STAGE

Reading the Book of Ruth, you can almost imagine poor, depressed Naomi suddenly slapping herself on the forehead as she realizes that Ruth has "accidentally" wandered into the field of her husband's relative, Boaz. It's as if Naomi has been so deep in her own sorrow and bitterness that she hadn't even begun to figure out what to do next.

In my experience, that's just when God tends to intervene in a way that supersedes my wildest imagination. It's as if he was waiting for me to give up my plans and my ideas for the future so he could sweep those inferior ideas out of the way and get on to the bigger vision. That's why I think mentoring is often something that happens to us, not something we set out to do. It's not like we hang out shingle to advertise, "Older woman wants to share experience." It's more like we get on our knees and ask God to show us how to be available.

Most women, I have found, have a very poor view of what their talents are and are typically insecure about what they have to offer. It's easy for those of us who have reached a certain age to feel unable to offer much to younger women or even to one another. But that's not a saintly attitude; it's a sense of false pride that doesn't want to be embarrassed. Often, the most important thing we have to offer is so obvious we don't even consider it.

Once Naomi "snapped out of it" and realized that God was still very involved in her and Ruth's lives, her instincts took over. After all these years of following the customs of Moab and watching her sons court women in a totally different way, she now was able to advise Ruth in the very customs her own mother had probably taught her. She remembered that there might be another relative more closely related than Boaz, so she advised Ruth to take things slowly. She knew how easily a beautiful foreign woman could gain a bad reputation.

Naomi knew that God was in control of the situation, so she continued to talk to him, even as she was advising Ruth about the customs and courting principles of her people. Perhaps she thought back to her own courting days

with Elimelech and spoke to Ruth out of her own experience. There is nothing to indicate that Naomi had to
search for answers or consult her friends about what to do.
She had the confidence that comes from being certain of
what she knows and under marching orders from God.

God is calling us women in the second half of life to
be encouragers and teachers to younger women. Maybe
it means he wants us to just provide a place and time to
meet. Perhaps he will call us to start a Bible study. Whatever the case, all he asks of us is an open heart and a
willingness to set aside the pride that says, "Oh I couldn't
possibly do that." Being a mentor doesn't need to be a
major undertaking. Often, it's just the willingness to put
your arm around a younger woman and tell her that
she's going to make it through this phase of life.

12. the story doesn't end

The Book of Ruth is a beautiful story of redemption, friendship, and God's grace. Not only is it theologically significant, but it is also considered one of the most literary books of the Bible. Benjamin Franklin, knowing the Book of Ruth well from his childhood, actually used it to play a prank on some French colleagues. It seems that when Franklin was serving in France, he overheard some Frenchmen dismissing the Bible as having no literary style. Although Franklin wasn't a believer in the Bible, he had grown up with it and felt the French were being snobs. So he took the Book of Ruth, changed all the proper nouns to French names, and wrote the story in longhand. The French read the story and declared it, "Charmant!" Franklin proved his point that the Bible was a book worthy of study by educated and sophisticated men.

One of the most beautiful aspects of this biblical story is the final scene. It might have been enough for Ruth to marry Boaz. The story could have ended there, and everyone would have still proclaimed it a book about redemption and loyalty. But the real ending comes when Ruth and Boaz have a son named Obed, and Naomi takes him in her lap and cares for him while all of her friends gather around.

You can almost imagine this as the final scene in a Broadway musical. Naomi sits center stage, with graying hair and face wrinkled in a magnificent smile. In her lap, baby Obed coos to her while a chorus of her women friends gather around singing. They sing the praises of Ruth, telling Naomi that her daughter-in-law was "worth more to you than seven sons!" (Ruth 4:15). Then they praise Boaz, the kinsman redeemer. They all lift up their voices and agree that there has never been a more perfect baby than Obed. Then they bring it all back to Naomi. Naomi has triumphed, not in any way she might have imagined but in a way so spectacular that only a chorus of praise can hint of the significance of Obed's birth. Naomi is now the great-great-grandmother of David. She has been grafted into the lineage of Jesus. The woman who once seemed so hopeless has found her very reason for living.

This is the highpoint of Naomi's life. Everything she did a the first half of her life, no matter how successful, couldn't

hold a candle to what God had done for her. Naomi didn't
know that she was holding the grandfather of King David,
of course. But she did know that despite all the trials, she
now had a family, a grandchild to love and care for, and
a future that was better than anything she had hoped for
when she was young.

MY OWN NAOMI

It's not easy to get to Pembine, Wisconsin. From Washington, D.C., it requires a flight to Chicago, then one to
Green Bay, and either a commuter flight to Iron Mountain,
Michigan, or a long drive. But because I wanted my two
boys to know their great-grandma Hanson, I loaded them
up and took them for a visit.

Grandma Hanson was in a nursing home, and I thought
it would lift her spirits to see my boys. Although we weren't
exactly sure when we would arrive, I told her that I would
see her sometime in the afternoon. So when we walked
into her room, I was surprised to find it empty. "Oh, she's
probably either at crafts, or maybe it's time for the Bible
study," the nurse told me, not at all surprised that my nine-
ty-two-year-old grandmother was missing. "She's a pretty
busy lady."

The boys and I went out to get something to eat and
returned an hour later. This time we found Grandma in
her room along with half a dozen other people. She was

glad to see us and pleased that we could meet her other visitors. She began introducing us, and I realized that her visitors included two college students, a middle-aged woman, and a young couple with their toddler. During the next two days of our visit, Grandma had many more visitors of all ages. They seemed to arrive at all times of the day, and not one of them seemed to be there because they were worried that my grandma was lonely. They came because they loved seeing her, were seeking her advice, or just wanted to spend some time with someone with twinkling blue eyes and a big smile.

Grandma seemed intimately aware of the details of their lives. She'd taught Sunday school for sixty years, and many of the adults who came to visit had first met her as children. She'd loved them through scraped knees and scrapes with the law. She'd gone to their weddings and watched them have children of their own. Some of them looked like they had just come from church, and some looked like they hadn't been to church for some time. (After one particularly tough-looking teenager left, she said, "He thinks he doesn't believe in the Lord anymore, but he'll come back.") I was amazed that such a wild-looking teen had taken the time to come to a nursing home to visit my grandma.

When it was time to leave, Grandma Hanson hugged us all and thanked us for coming. She was grateful for our visit, but we were even more grateful for having spent the time with such a remarkable woman. The older I get, the more I realize how truly remarkable Grandma Hanson really was.

She had very little education and never traveled out of the Midwest. She had lived mostly in small towns, and her résumé consisted of raising four boys, acres of vegetables, and an assortment of chickens, cows, pigs, and goats in order to feed the family. Grandma had no power, little money, and none of what the world would consider success. Yet in her nineties, widowed and surviving two of her four sons, she was one of the most popular residents of the nursing home. People went out of their way to visit her, and she was loved and valued for who she was and what she had given to so many.

My grandma has been gone for some time now, but I carry that image of her with me. The photos of Grandma in the nursing home, arthritis-crippled arms around each of her great-grandsons, are prominent in the albums I have made for each of them. My sons have both heard many stories about Grandma Hanson because I want them to remember their spiritual legacy. She was the one who, as the young mother of four boys, married to an alcoholic husband, and feeling hopeless about her life, took her children to a nearby church and came to know God in a way that changed her and her sons. Eventually, Grandpa Hanson came around, too, and they spent much of their married life doing "the Lord's work" either as volunteers or as caretakers of a Christian camp.

Our family can trace our spiritual roots back to this humble woman, and I like reminding my sons that one person's decisions can influence the next generations. We have so much, thanks to Grandma Hanson.

FINISHING WELL

A common principle of good management is, "Begin with the end in mind." The point is simply to know where you want to end up so you keep aiming in the right direction. I am now at a place in life where I take seriously what I once thought were silly questions like, "What would you want your tombstone to say?" I am beginning to think about my own legacy.

Since my local newspaper is the *Washington Post*, I get a daily dose of famous obituaries mixed in with those of ordinary people. Sometimes the famous people's obituaries contain so many titles and appointments that I wonder if they simply died from exhaustion. Sometimes the so-called ordinary people are shown to be extraordinary after all. Yesterday, I read about a man who had invented the intermittent windshield wiper and then spent the rest of his life fighting for the right to claim the innovation as his own. Another day, I read about a woman who had been the longtime editor of a style manual I once used faith-fully. Perhaps I will still invent something or become an editor again. But what I really want is to end up like Grandma Hanson, still so full of life and interested in other people that I am giving to others with my very last breath.

I spent much time taking in during the first decades of my life. I used to laugh when I saw the bumper sticker, "He who dies with the most toys wins." Now I think it is ter-ribly sad to think of people who still value toys when they die. I am trying to unload as much as I can, mentally and physically. For the first time in my life, I see possessions as burdens and relationships as blessings.

When my father was first diagnosed with a fatal brain tumor, he acted consistent with his responsible nature: he began to clean out his closet and give away his clothes. It was his attempt to control what he could, an act of concern for my mother, so she wouldn't have to take care of it after he was gone. I look at the piles in my office and closet, and I pray I don't die suddenly. My sons would spend months getting rid of all the stuff. "Mom was such a pack rat," I imagine them saying.

It's time for me to start paring down. All those things I have kept for "someday" are just in the way of today. And I am more convinced than ever that I have no idea what the future holds.

INVESTING FOR THE FUTURE

A few years ago, I was attending a publishing conference, and a friend offered me a ride to the airport so we could get a few minutes to catch up on old times during the drive. As we were about to leave, the doorman from the hotel stopped us and said that the hotel bus had broken down. Would we mind taking another passenger to the airport? We were less than cheerful about it since we had hoped to spend that time in conversation, but we agreed, and the man jumped in the back seat with thanks.

My friend Bruce asked the man where he worked, and he mentioned the name of a Christian publishing house affiliated with a campus organization. "I have really fond memories of that group," my friend Bruce said, "because I attended a weekend retreat one time, and that's where I became a Christian. It was in 1972 in New Hampshire."

Bruce went on to explain that he had not only become a Christian that weekend, but a year later when he gave his testimony, his entire family came to the Lord. His sister eventually became a Wycliffe missionary and translated Scripture for a people group in Africa. His parents turned their publishing interests to Christian books and published some of the biggest Christian books of the next decades. Bruce had become publisher of a major Christian publishing house and brought many significant Christian books to the public. The impact of that retreat had reverberated throughout the world.

We waited for the man to respond, but he was silent. Maybe we were boring him, we thought. Then we realized he was stunned. He stuttered as he broke the silence. "I led that retreat," he said. "It was my first time as a conference leader, and I felt like a total failure. Until this moment, I have always believed it was one of the biggest failures of my life."

By the time we reached the airport, we all had tears in our eyes. What had seemed like the simple act of offering a ride to a stranger had turned into a powerful reminder that God uses our efforts whether we realize it or not. I've often heard, "We're called to be faithful, not successful." But I don't think I've ever experienced such an obvious example of God revealing the truth of that statement until that day.

I may spend the rest of my life doing things that don't seem at all successful. Yet only God knows the purpose. I am called simply to be faithful.

Recently, I was asked to speak to a group of leaders about the global AIDS crisis. I was thrilled that this group was willing to take the time to hear about such an important issue and I prepared thoroughly for my talk and for what I anticipated to be a stimulating question-and-answer session. The group was polite and attentive, but when it came to the question time, they had none. It wasn't as if the topic had been thoroughly covered in my brief talk. It occurred to me, as I looked at them, that they simply weren't interested. I was disappointed and exasperated.

Later, I sent an e-mail to Kay Warren, who has spent so much of her time trying to help people understand the global AIDS crisis. She also had been speaking at a conference about AIDS. I told her of my experience and asked about hers. Her response was a good and godly reminder: "It's not my concern to figure out the work of the Spirit . . . merely to do my part." She was so right. Doing what we are called to do is the point.

VISIONS OF HELL

God's economy is not the same as ours. In fact, some of the happiest people I've ever met are living in physical circumstances more devastating than anything I could even imagine—such as the man in Goma, Congo, whose unwavering faith and joy reminded me that God is writing a story so much bigger than my clouded vision can see.

This is exactly what hell will look like, I thought as I stood on the still-steaming lava in what once was the main street of Goma, Congo. The smell of sulphur choked my nose and throat and lava still bubbled up through deep crevices around us. The volcano that had spewed this destruction on Goma had stopped erupting a month before, but the crust was still so hot that we couldn't leave our car sitting for long or the tires would blow out. Our feet hurt if we stood still too long as the heat went through the soles of even our sturdiest shoes.

Downtown Goma was obliterated; buried under ten feet of molten rock. A few roofs of buildings that had second stories peeked out of the smoldering mess. A billboard proclaiming Internet Café stood above the river of prehistoric rock. Even the hospital, farther away from town, now held only singed and melted equipment and lava that had flowed and hardened in odd shapes.

Surprisingly, no one had been killed. The volcano erupted at night, but it made a huge show before belching out the fire. The warning was enough for the people closest to the mountain to flee. Those who lived in town had time to pack up a few things before running toward the lake where they might eventually have to seek refuge if the lava flow continued for long. Some people returned to find their houses still standing, lava flows splitting and going around random buildings while incinerating all the others.

I sat in a refugee camp with people who had nowhere to go. Nothing would grow on the lava, and they couldn't dig through it. They would have to find another place to live, but they had nothing. A woman held a baby whose hand was badly burned. I searched my backpack for the small tube of ointment I carried, giving it to her and showing her how to put it on her baby's wound. She thanked me profusely. A little boy came up to me, trying to sell me a toy he had fashioned out of the bands from the bundles holding supplies for the refugee camp. It was a truck, with wheels cut from the rubber soles of flip-flops. He asked for a dollar. I gave him two and nearly started a riot among the other children.

Someone pulled on my arm and told me in French that there was a man I should meet. I found him reading out loud in the midst of a group of people crowding around to hear. He was at least seventy years old and wearing a tattered t-shirt and pants that couldn't have been his own. He interrupted his reading to greet me and tell me his story. He was one of the people who lived near the volcano, so he had little warning. He fled in only his underwear, but he took one thing that was always near his bed. He held up the book that was so well worn I hadn't recognized it until that moment. With a huge smile on his face, he told me that God had spared his life and his Bible. "Surely I am the most fortunate man on earth!" he declared.

I will not soon forget that man, sitting in that awful place, everything he owned destroyed and little hope for a promising future. He was one of the happiest people I have ever met. He was thoroughly content to sit in a dreary refuge camp, reading his Bible to anyone who would listen. He did not ask me for help or a handout. He did ask if I wanted to sit and listen with the others. And so I sat with mostly dirty and exhausted refugees, listening to God's Word and learning again that God is truly sufficient for our every need.

A MOUNTAINTOP EXPERIENCE

My visit to the Karen village in Thailand brought another surprising ending. After watching the process of helping build the official identities of the people in the village, our group was tired. We were shown to a one-room building, the villagers' community center, where we would all sleep on the floor. We were starting to open our sleeping bags when we heard the whispers. The villagers were gathering outside the door for some sort of meeting. We quickly moved our belongings out of the way to accommodate them.

We assumed the villagers were Buddhist, as were most of the hill tribes of Thailand. But in this particular village, we were surprised to discover that the villagers were coming to hold their weekly church service. They were Christians and wondered if we would join them for worship. We were thrilled.

One of the visitors preached a brief sermon in Thai that was then translated to the local dialect. Although we couldn't understand any of the words, we watched the beautiful faces of the villagers illuminated by candlelight and understood how much they appreciated hearing God's Word.

Then we began to sing. The songs they knew were the familiar songs of faith. "Holy, Holy, Holy." "Blessed Be the Tie that Binds." "Amazing Grace." We sang in English, the IJM staff in Thai, and the villagers in the Karen dialect. Here we were, on the top of the mountain in a remote village, singing familiar songs in communion with brothers and sisters in Christ. We all had tears in our eyes as we sang, our voices making us feel like we had everything in common.

Later, it occurred to me to ask how these remote villagers knew these traditional hymns of the faith. They were in such a remote location that outsiders had only recently entered their village. Few of them could read or write. There were no telephones or radios. And they lived in an overwhelmingly Buddhist region.

When I asked one of the Thai staff, she said, "They probably brought their faith with them." When I asked her to explain, she told me that this village was descended from Burmese immigrants who had fled to these mountains. Burma is a country now closed to missionaries, but for a time, a generation ago, it was open, and the missionaries who taught there left a lasting legacy of faith. Perhaps a hundred years before, a missionary had told one person in

Burma about Jesus. Perhaps she never even knew if her words made a difference. But here, in the remote hills of Thailand, an entire village worshiped the Lord.

HOW THEN SHALL WE LIVE?

Only God knows how my story will end. My spiritual obituary may be very different from the notice that appears in a newspaper. Spiritually, I would like it to read, "She was faithful." But I know, even as I write that, that I will be tempted to settle for a list of accomplishments instead. I will still want to measure faithfulness by success. I will still be tempted to think that I am not doing enough when God asks me to be still and listen.

I know I am called to pray and live in the present. I believe God asks me to have fellowship with friends and to give back to others. I know that I am to trust in his vision for the rest of my life and to live in faith even when I don't see evidence of his hand at work.

I am called to live like Naomi—humbly, faithfully, fully. I am called to something so much greater than I can imagine that I pray for the courage to face the adventure God has for me in the second half of my life. My purpose is being revealed each day as I follow God's lead.

I live expectantly, trying to tame my own ambitions so they won't obscure what God has for me. I live passionately, knowing that God's will for me is not a passing phase or

216 second calling

an emotional high. And I live meaningfully, knowing that God has a call on my life that is stronger, deeper, and richer than anything that came before.

My prayer is that more and more women will embrace their own second calling in a way that is not only personally life-changing but powerfully world-changing.

notes

Chapter 1: A New Day Dawning

1. Bob Buford, *Halftime* (Grand Rapids: Zondervan, 1995); *Game Plan: Winning Strategies for the Second Half of Your Life* (Grand Rapids: Zondervan, 1997).

2. C. S. Jung, "Stages of Life," *The Structure and Dynamics of the Psyche* (New York: Bollingen, 1970).

3. Emilie Griffin, *Clinging: The Experience of Prayer* (New York: Harper & Row, 1984).

Chapter 2: Getting Personal

1. Judith Viorst, *Necessary Losses: The Loves, Illusions, Dependencies, and Impossible Expectations That All of Us Have to Give Up in Order to Grow* (New York: Fireside, 1998), 269, 267.

2. From the 2000 U.S. Census report, "Age Groups and Sex," Summary File 1.

3. Diane Brady with Brian Grow, "Act II," *Business Week*, 29 March 2004.

Chapter 3: What Really Counts

1. Stephen R. Covey, *The Seven Habits of Highly Effective People* (New York: Simon & Schuster, 1990).

2. Parker J. Palmer, *Let Your Life Speak: Listening for the Voice of Vocation* (New York: Jossey-Bass, 1999).

3. Ibid., 16.

4. Laurie Beth Jones, *The Path: Creating Your Mission Statement for Work and for Life* (New York: Hyperion, 1998).

5. Oswald Chambers, *My Utmost for His Highest*, January 23, public domain.

Chapter 4: Making Peace with the Past

1. Richard Rohr, *Everything Belongs: The Gift of Contemplative Prayer* (New York: Crossroad, 1999), 43.

2. Byron Katie with Stephen Mitchell, *Loving What Is: Four Questions That Can Change Your Life* (New York: Three Rivers Press, 2003). This five-step process is not identified with any religion, Christian or otherwise; Katie's web site clarifies that she "developed The Work completely out of her own experiences. Any similarities to other systems [of belief] are purely coincidental." The author's

personal experience with The Work does not constitute an endorsement of *Loving What Is*, Byron Katie. or her recommended resources.

3. I have changed the name and circumstances of this example to purposely obscure the person's identity. What is important is the change that occurred in my way of thinking, so I do not want to embarrass anyone involved in the actual situation.

4. Chris Thurman, *The Lies We Believe* (Nashville: Thomas Nelson, 2003), 5.

Chapter 5: Leaving the Baggage Behind

1. Henry Cloud and John Townsend, *God Will Make a Way: What to Do When You Don't Know What to Do* (Nashville: Integrity, 2002), 28–29.

2. Beth Moore, *Praying God's Word: Breaking Free from Spiritual Strongholds* (Nashville: Broadman & Holman, 2000).

3. Dale Hanson Bourke and Dr. Linda Smoling Moore, adapted from Alcoholics Anonymous materials.

4. Daniel G. Amen, *Change Your Brain, Change Your Life: The Breakthrough Program for Conquering Anxiety, Depression, Obsessiveness, Anger, and Impulsiveness* (New York: Three Rivers Press, 1999).

5. Daniel G. Amen, *Healing the Hardware of Your Soul: How Making the Brain-Soul Connection Can Optimize Your Life, Love, and Spiritual Growth* (New York: Free Press, 2002).

6. Richard Rohr, *Everything Belongs: The Gift of Contemplative Prayer* (New York: Crossroad, 1999), 52.

7. Sue Monk Kidd, *When the Heart Waits: Spiritual Direction for Life's Sacred Questions* (San Francisco: HarperSanFrancisco, 1992), 27–28.

Chapter 6: **Giving Up Idols**

1. Gerald May, *Addiction and Grace* (San Francisco: HarperSanFrancisco, 1991), 13.

2. Ward Brehm, *White Man Walking: An American Businessman's Spiritual Adventure in Africa* (Minneapolis: Kirk House, 2003), 105.

3. Larry Crabb, *Inside Out* (Colorado Springs: NavPress, 1988), 87.

Chapter 7: **A New Identity**

1. Dale Hanson Bourke, "Jill Briscoe: God's Dynamic Entrepreneur" *Today's Christian Woman*, Jan/Feb 1989.

2. Ibid.

3. Parker J. Palmer, *Let Your Life Speak: Listening for the Voice of Vocation* (New York: Jossey-Bass, 1999), 12.

Chapter 8: **Without a Prayer**

1. Signa Bodishbaugh, *The Journey to Wholeness in Christ: A Devotional Adventure to Becoming Whole* (Grand Rapids: Chosen, 1997), 25.

2. Richard Wagner, *Christian Prayer for Dummies* (New York: Wiley Publishing, 2003).

3. Dale Hanson Bourke, *The Skeptics Guide to the Global AIDS Crisis: Tough Questions, Direct Answers* (Atlanta: Authentic, 2004).

Chapter 10: **Living in the Present**

1. Richard Rohr, *Everything Belongs: The Gift of Contemplative Prayer* (New York: Crossroad, 1999), 29.

Chapter 11: **Passing It On**

1. Anne Ortlund, *Discipling One Another* (Dallas: Word Publishing, 1983).